Transition:
A guide to climbing real rock

Transition:
A guide to climbing real rock

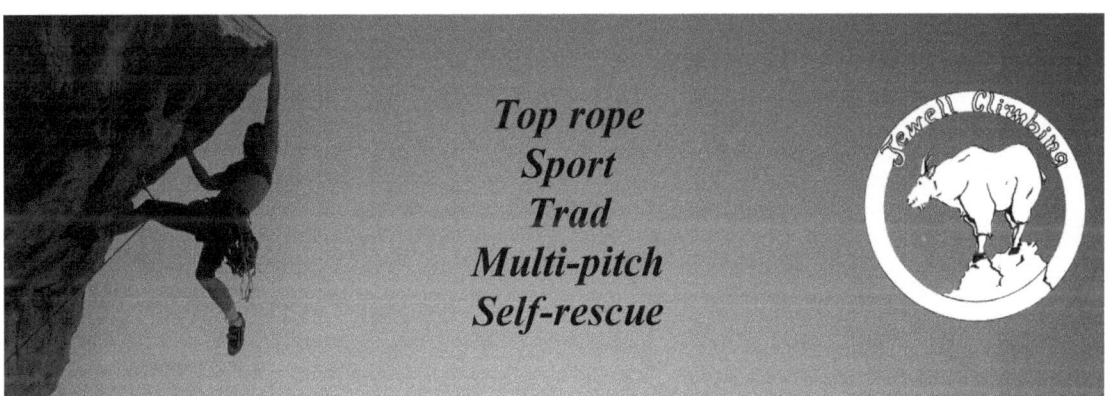

Top rope
Sport
Trad
Multi-pitch
Self-rescue

Mark Davidson Jewell

Dedicated to Karl Seidenschmid, my uncle who taught me to climb

Thank you to Mike Adolphe and the ACMG, Éric Lachance and the FQME, Marc-Etienne Brunet and Oli Watt-Meyer for their comments on the manuscript, and Simone Poirier, Adolphe Ridel-Brouillard, Nader Mohamed Zébib, Joanie Pelletier and Marianne Laliberté for help with photography.

Second Edition
Copyright © 2021 by Mark Davidson Jewell

All rights reserved. No part of this book may be reproduced or transmitted in any form by any means, electronic or mechanical, including photocopying and recording, or by any information storage and retrieval system, except as may be expressly permitted in writing by the author.

Editor: Ross Curtner
Cover design: Guy Bouchard

Photos by the author, unless otherwise specified
Illustrations by Marion Bouchard

ISBN 9781777 375904

Warning: Climbing is a dangerous sport. You can be seriously injured or die. Read the following before you use this book.

The material presented in this book is the result of research done by various reputable climbing organisations such as the FQME, UIAA and ACMG as well as my own opinions. Explanations are brief as this book is intended to complement in-person instruction. It is therefore not in itself adequate to replace formal instruction from a qualified guide. Climbing is inherently dangerous and in practicing the sport you accept responsibility for your own safety and assume the risk of injury or death. The author assumes no liability for accidents or injuries sustained by readers who engage in activities described in this book.

INTRODUCTION 9
Hazards, risk and decision making 9
Environmental concerns 11
Ethics, Style and Etiquette 13

CHAPTER 1 - BASIC EQUIPMENT 17
Nylon material 18
Harness 19
Rope 20
Slings, webbing and runners 24
Cordelette 26
Personal tether 26
Helmet 27
Carabiners 27
Quicklinks 30
Belay devices 30
Bolts 32

CHAPTER 2 – KNOTS AND HITCHES 35

CHAPTER 3 – TOP ROPE 41
Scouting the anchor position 41
Anchor basics 43
Anchor-building on bolts 46
Anchor-building on trees 51
Ground anchors 55
The rule of redundancy 56
Rappelling 56
Climbing and belaying 57
Cleaning the belay anchor 63
Essential equipment checklist 66

CHAPTER 4 – SINGLE-PITCH SPORT CLIMBING 67
Differences between leading inside and outside 67
Before leaving the ground 68
Clipping 69
Footwork 70
Lead belaying 71
Forces and physics 72
What to do once at the top 76
To rappel or to lower 82
Cleaning draws 83
Bailing off a bolt 84
Essential equipment checklist 86

CHAPTER 5 – MULTI-PITCH SPORT CLIMBING 87
- Preparation 87
- Multi-pitch belay anchors 87
- Belaying from above 89
- Sequences, communication, transitions 94
- Avoiding a factor two fall 95
- Climbing as a party of three 96
- Multi-pitch rappelling 97
- Final considerations 100
- Essential equipment checklist 100

CHAPTER 6 – SELF-RESCUE 101
- Basics 101
- Friction hitches 102
- Catastrophe knots 103
- Getting hands free 104
- Escaping the Belay 106
- Rescuing yourself 110
- Rescuing the second 115
- Passing knots 123
- Compound rappels 124
- Rescuing the leader 128
- Overview of rescue sequences 131

CHAPTER 7 - TRADITIONAL CLIMBING 133
- Placing protection 133
- Leading on gear 141
- Advanced belaying 151
- Traditional belay anchors 151

APPENDIX 1 – ENGLISH-FRENCH TRANSLATION OF TECHNICAL TERMS 163

APPENDIX 2 – ENGLISH-FRENCH TRANSLATION OF COMMANDS 165

CLIMBERS' CODE OF RESPECT

Educate yourself about outdoor rock climbing ethics, safety considerations and how to lessen your environmental impact at the cliff.

ROCKRESPECT

RESPECT THE DANGERS

- Learn necessary outdoor climbing skills from a guide/mentor
- Learn about the cliff: protection/difficulty/hazards
- Wear a helmet, rocks can break, yell "rock" if rock/gear falls
- Inspect/clean your gear often, replace when worn/expired
- Triple check and back up your systems (harness/knot/belay/rappel/anchor)
- Communicate with your partner and other climbers
- Learn how to detect if fixed gear/bolts are safe

RESPECT THE ENVIRONMENT

- Stay on designated trails to lessen impact
- Pack out your trash and pick up after others
- Use existing bathroom facilities or dig a hole, bury it, and pack out toilet paper
- **Do not** feed or hurt animals
- Place boulder pads/backpack on non-vegetated surfaces
- **Do not** damage/chip the rock. Brush off your tick marks
- Be aware of seasonal fire bans and follow regulations

RESPECT OTHERS

- Climb in smaller groups. Share climbs with others
- Check if dogs are allowed, keep dogs leashed
- Pull your ropes when finished. Yell "rope" when pulling ropes
- Keep noise levels appropriate, no loud music/profanities
- Respect "right of way" on multi-pitch/shared anchors

RESPECT CLIMBING ACCESS

- Respect land owner rules or provincial/federal regulations
- **Do not** leave gear unless permitted
- Park considerately, carpool if possible
- Camp only in designated/permitted areas
- Respect area closures (seasonal/permanent)
- Pay required entrance fees/permits
- Follow Transport Canada regulations for drone use

In collaboration with

PLEASE VISIT ROCKRESPECT.CA FOR MORE INFO

Introduction

The joy of dancing up a warm rock face is like none other, and to do so with confidence and autonomy, within a reasonable margin of safety created by one's own decision making, is the aspiration of every climber. The aim of this book is to present a concise, yet comprehensive overview of the skills needed to climb outdoors safely. It is intended for those who already climb inside on artificial walls and are making the transition to outdoor top rope, sport, or traditional climbing. It should serve as a review for those who have completed a transition course, helping to solidify theoretical knowledge to be applied to real situations.

Chapters are progressive, each containing essential information for those that follow. To keep the book concise, material is rarely repeated. For this reason, it is strongly recommended to read the chapters sequentially, confirming autonomy in each discipline before moving on to the next.

Hazards, risk and decision making

Unlike the climbing gym, the outdoor environment is uncontrolled. There are no tests to pass, no one to verify your equipment, no one to scold you for reckless behaviour. You are completely responsible for yourself. To many this freedom is the appeal of rock climbing. While there are of course many skills and techniques to master in order to safely make the transition from gym climbing to rock climbing, the most important change is a mental shift; developing awareness of risks and learning to constantly assess one's situation and surroundings. There may be several risks present simultaneously, both at the micro and macro levels, that require you make judgement calls and create management systems to deal with them. This is especially true for traditional climbing where the leader is building anchor systems while climbing, although it is also the case in even the simplest top rope scenarios. Risk assessment and management are the most important skills to learn as a new rock climber, but ironically, are the hardest to learn without experience. This book is my attempt at passing on this experience.

Let's begin with a few definitions. Simply put, a hazard is a source of potential danger. Building on this, a risk incorporates the probability of encountering this danger and can be thought of as the product of the consequence and the probability of encountering a hazard. Risk management, then, is a systematic approach that seeks to reduce or nullify the probability of coming into contact with, or to reduce the severity of hazards present in a given environment.

A situation that is risky for one person might be relatively safe for another if they are able to keep the likelihood of encountering hazards low. In addition, every climber has a different level of risk that they deem acceptable. Most pitches of climbing, from top rope to trad, will involve sections where a fall would be dangerous. For example, on a top rope climb, rope stretch usually results in a ground fall if the climber falls during the first few meters of the route. This could pose a considerable hazard if the landing is uneven with sharp boulders. If the beginning of the route is well within the climber's ability, they may deem this risk acceptable because of the low probability of encountering the hazard. However, a second climber may find the start of the route at the limit of their ability and choose to use either a spotter, crash pads or both to protect the landing, decreasing the severity of the hazard to compensate for the increased probability of encountering it. A third climber, not willing to accept the possibility of spraining an ankle, may deem the risk too high and choose to avoid the route altogether. There are few hard rules governing how to manage risks, but rather principles that, when combined with sound

INTRODUCTION

judgment, enable climbers to reduce the risk to a level they deem acceptable and within a margin of error.

Objective and subjective hazards

Categorizing potential risks into objective and subjective hazards can help us better understand the nature of these risks and come up with appropriate strategies to reduce or mitigate them. Objective hazards are those that are mostly out of our control, usually related to the environment. These include loose rock, rock fall, bad weather, dangerous approach and descent trails, etc. For example, suppose we are confronted with a section of cliff with increased likelihood of rockfall due to poor rock quality and the presence of several overhead parties. We could reduce the probability of coming in contact with this objective hazard by moving quickly through the dangerous terrain, we could reduce the consequence of this hazard by wearing a helmet, or we could nullify this hazard by finding a different path altogether.

Subjective hazards are those related to factors introduced by the climber and include everything from dehydration due to poor preparation to rappelling off the ends of the rope due to sloppy practices and lack of attention. To reduce and manage these risks, we rely on good judgement, constant vigilance, the rule of redundancy, and systematic double checking. For example, imagine a runout section on a traditional lead. The hazard is a potentially dangerous lead fall where if the last piece of protection were to fail, the climber could hit a ledge. The presence of the ledge is an objective hazard, but the amount of gear placed is subjective. The hazard becomes a risk when combined with the probability of the leader falling. The leader may reduce the consequence of this risk by placing additional protection points to protect the climbing. However, if the climber determines that this gear needs to be conserved for higher up on the pitch, they may instead choose to reduce only the probability of falling by climbing in a controlled and conservative manner with a "no-fall" mindset. Finally, they may judge the risk too great and choose to lower off their highest protection piece and send their partner up instead to give the pitch a go, maybe after backcleaning lower protection.

What makes risk management difficult in climbing is that the different possible measures to reduce the probability or consequence of a risk often trade off against each other. For example, placing more protection low on a pitch reduces risk in the immediate but will increase risk significantly if the leader runs out of necessary gear higher up on the lead. Similarly, moving too quickly through an active rockfall area increases the probability of slipping, introducing another hazard. With experience, climbers can learn to integrate several risks simultaneously and make calm and thoughtful decisions based on sound judgement.

Risk management is often complicated by fear which clouds judgement. Climbers must learn to assess risk rationally despite instinctive emotional responses. This means not feeding fear when a rational assessment has deemed the level of risk acceptable but also not pushing through fear without acknowledging its source. By understanding fear but without fixating on it we can free up our mental energies for the climbing itself.

The following is a non-exhaustive list of important hazards (both objective and subjective) to consider that don't apply to gym climbing:

- Bad weather, including lightning
- Rock fall (natural or human-caused)
- Dangers around cliff edge
- Sharp rock edges that can damage or cut the rope
- Damaged equipment (you're responsible for inspecting everything)
- Anchor failure
- Lowering or rappelling off the end of a rope that is too short for the climb

INTRODUCTION

- Dangerous climber falls (protruding ledges, pendulums, long leader falls etc.)
- Sloping or dangerous belay terrain
- Sparsely spaced bolts (sport climbing)
- Unexpected runouts (trad climbing)
- Lack of cell phone coverage in the case of an emergency
- Wiping one's arse with poison ivy

This book aims to clearly present the risks associated with different styles of rock climbing and equip the reader with the necessary skills to manage them effectively. However, staying safe while climbing ultimately depends on the quality of your judgement and decision making and can't be guaranteed by simply following the rules or guidelines in this book. Part of what makes rock climbing engaging and satisfying over the long term is that it involves continuous learning and with this gained experience comes greater freedom to climb in more complex situations with confidence and pleasure.

Environmental concerns

For many, part of the draw of rock climbing is that it brings us into intimate proximity with nature. The forest solitude, the views of the landscape, feeling the fine contours of the earth's bare skeleton under our hands and feet as we climb and enjoying the diversity of plants, lichens and animals that inhabit these seemingly inhospitable places, all enrich the climbing experience. Cliff, alpine and sub-alpine ecosystems are all extremely fragile, easily disturbed and slow to recover. Given the scarcity of soil, plants must struggle to anchor themselves and uptake water and nutrients. This can result in extraordinarily slow growth rates and thus surprisingly long-lived individuals. The small stunted Eastern White Cedars growing from cracks and on ledges of the Niagara escarpment, a popular climbing site in Ontario, are as old as 1000 years, the oldest trees in Eastern North America.

Eastern white cedar (Thuja occidentalis) growing on the Niagara escarpment. Photo: Peter Kelly

Umbilicarian lichens, the rock tripes that grow on many cliffs and boulders, may be as old as 100 years when about the size of the palm of your hand, and crustose lichens often scrubbed off climbing routes may in some cases be thousands of years old, amongst the oldest organisms (they're actually symbiotic partnerships, not organisms) on earth!

Smooth rock tripe (Umbilicaria mamulata)

INTRODUCTION

Crustose lichens may be thousands of years old, and are used to date rocks and glacial movement

The hardy species that live in these ecosystems, as well as being easily disturbed and slow to recover, are often rare and endemic, meaning that they grow here and only here. Since these species then have nowhere else to go, depending on cliffs as their unique habitat, as climbing expands over a larger and larger percentage of potential habitat sites, certain species may be put at risk.

Recent studies have investigated the impact of climbing on plant biodiversity by comparing climbed to unclimbed sections of cliff. Results suggest that climbing, as well as unsurprisingly reducing overall abundance of vegetation, may also reduce plant diversity considerably as well as increase the presence of non-native invasive species that can quickly propagate into such disturbed habitats. What this means is that the old saying of "take nothing but photos, leave nothing but footprints," must be applied even more strictly for climbers, since even footprints in fragile ecosystems, when there are enough of them, can have a significant impact.

Besides vegetation, there are a number of animal species that depend on cliff habitats for reproduction and survival. Notably among these are several species of predatory birds who must be taken into special consideration. The Peregrine falcon for example, once critically endangered due to DDT use in the 1960s, uses vertical cliffs as nesting sites. If climbers get too close, parents may abandon their nests and offspring completely. It may also be in your own interest to stay away since an encounter with a vicious bird of prey protecting their young against an intruder could result in a dangerous encounter. Cliff sections in falcon habitat may close seasonally if nests are spotted. It is critical that we respect these closures to help populations recover. Although still listed as a species of "special concern" by the IUCN (International Union for the Conservation of Nature), falcon conservation efforts are a success story as populations have recovered from the brink of extinction to healthy and stable numbers, with much monitoring done by or in collaboration with the climbing community.

Peregrine falcon (Falco peregrinus)

Back when climbing was practised by only a handful of eccentric recluses, impact on the environment was negligible. But now with climbing skyrocketing in popularity, it is increasingly important that we cultivate a culture of low-impact use and stewardship. Not only must we take responsibility for our own actions and do everything possible to reduce our impact, we must also take responsibility collectively for the entire climbing community, leaving climbing sites cleaner than when we found them, encouraging good practises within our groups and getting involved in and supporting conservation initiatives.

List of good practices

Approach:
- Hike in small groups
- Stay on trails, don't cut corners
- Walk in single file if the trail is narrow
- Walk through mud, not around it, to avoid widening the path and accelerating erosion

When nature calls:
- If there is no outhouse, bury your turds in a cathole dug 15-20 cm deep, at least 60m from any water body. Keep a garden trowel in your pack for this. Burn, bury or pack out toilet paper.
- If in an alpine environment where decomposition rates are slow, pack it out
- On multi-pitch routes, never pee in cracks as they will remain eternally stinky. If necessary, pee on the rock face (off of the route) as it will both dry faster and get washed away more readily by rain. Pack your poop out.

Camping:
- Use designated camping areas, don't make new ones
- Be careful not to spill food during preparation. Clean it up if you do.
- Don't bury uneaten food; animals will dig it up. Pack it out instead.
- Store food securely when away from camp
- Pack out all garbage
- In high-use areas, avoid cutting or even gathering wood for fires. Use a backpacking stove instead.
- Cook on rock, gravel or snow instead of on vegetated areas
- Pick up what others may have left behind

Cliff base:
- Don't clear or cut away vegetation
- Don't turn over boulders which disturbs habitat

Cliff face:
- Respect closures, for example due to bird nesting
- Use less chalk. Chalk, when it's washed down the cliff by rain may alter pH and change nutrient availability for the plants growing there.

Cliff edge:
- Avoid walking on sections of eroding ground
- Avoid slinging trees if possible
- If rappelling off a tree, be sure to leave webbing or cordelette and a quicklink instead of passing your rope directly around the tree which will damage its bark

Other:
- Pack out what you pack in
- Pick up any garbage left by others
- Never feed the wildlife

Ethics, Style and Etiquette

As the cliché goes, climbing is not about getting to the top. Most of the time you could simply walk (or even drive) to reach the top of the wall. Alternatively, you could bolt in a via ferrata and climb a steel ladder to the summit. Clearly, the way in which you choose to climb a route is essential to the meaning associated with the ascent. This falls into the domain of ethics, style and etiquette. Although the essentials are briefly summarized here, norms often vary substantially between local climbing communities. When visiting a new site, to get an idea of what is accepted and expected, you should chat with local climbers and read published guidebooks which often include a section on local culture and standards.

Ethics

Climbing ethics involve choices made by the climbing community that will change the

INTRODUCTION

experience of future climbers. It involves any decisions related to permanent changes to the rock and largely revolves around bolting practises. Ethics vary to an alarming degree at the local scale and what is acceptable in one place may be a crime elsewhere. When and how to bolt has been the central ethical issue since the 1990s and remains so today. There is a general consensus that climbing should develop so as to promote safe practises, all the while preserving the rock for future generations and lessening environmental impact. The conflict is that to some, liberal bolting is seen to contribute to these objectives while to others it stands in stark opposition.

Style

Climbing style refers to the way in which a climber chooses to ascend a route and although can greatly affect the experience of that climber, has no concrete impact on how the route will be climbed in the future. As with climbing ethics, there is enormous variability at the local scale as to what styles are valued and idealised or scorned. There was a time when training in a gym for a route was considered "cheating" and using chalk poor style. To some, the purest style will always be a barefoot free solo by moonlight in their birthday suit.

Perhaps the biggest stylistic distinction is between top rope and lead climbing. Top rope is practised with the climber's rope running up through an anchor installed at the top of the route, and then back down to the belayer, whereas lead climbing involves the leader anchoring their rope into intermediate protection points as they climb. Since lead climbing involves climbing above your protection, it results in larger potential falls and therefore requires more commitment and caution. Lead climbing is practised in one of two main styles which concern the type of lead protection used. In sport climbing, the leader clips their rope to permanent bolts drilled into the rock whereas in traditional climbing, the leader places their own temporary and removable protection in natural cracks in the rock. Mixed climbing uses both bolts and traditional gear for protection. Whereas whether or not to drill bolts when opening a new route is an ethical consideration, whether or not to clip them as you climb is a stylistic one.

Free climbing and aid climbing can be contrasted in their extremes by free soloing on one hand with no rope and no safety equipment, and direct aid on the other with the leader drilling in bolt after bolt to construct a permanent ladder up the wall. In reality, nearly all climbing happens somewhere between these extremes and what constitutes "free climbing" can be controversial. Free climbing essentially refers to a style where all upward progress is achieved with the use of only the climber's hands and feet (and other body parts) while the rope and the protection system only serve to protect the climber from a potential fall, whereas aid climbing is the practise of engineering your way up a route with the help of your equipment. (Note that clean aid refers to aid climbing but without the use of bolts or pitons so as to preserve the rock). But does it count as "free" if you use a tree as a foot hold? Or what about stepping on the bolt hanger? Or what if you rest on a gear placement by holding onto a quickdraw a second too long as you clip it? The devil is in the details. Halfway between free and aid climbing is "French freeing", a somewhat derogatory term used to describe the style of making efficient upward progress by combining free moves with shamelessly pulling on gear to quickly move past hard sections.

The first major stylistic debates were waged in Yosemite over how to best climb the valley big walls. A longer route may be done with siege tactics involving fixing ropes so that the party can rappel to the ground or between established camps to sleep after pushing their highpoint and slowly make progress this way. The 1000m wall of El Capitan was first climbed in this style in 1958 by a team led by Warren Harding. It took them 47 days over an 18-month period. Siege tactics contrast with the "light and fast" style which minimizes the use of fixed ropes and instead makes upward progress in a single push. Both siege tactics and light and fast climbing can be applied to either aid or free climbing, though aid easily turns into a siege and free climbing is the most fun when it's done light.

There exist several terms to further describe the style in which a route is free climbed. First of all, to "send" or to "free" a route refers simply to free climbing it, climbing from the bottom to the top in one go without weighting the rope or gear. Applied to a multi-pitch climb, sending the route refers to sending all of the pitches on it without returning to the ground, regardless of whether all pitches are freed consecutively or with failed attempts between. "Onsight" refers to sending a route ground up, first try with no previous information (called "beta") about the route. With the popularity of in-depth guidebooks, online climbing forums and videos, and chalk trails from previous ascents, some argue that onsight no longer exists as a style. To "flash" a route means to send it ground up first try but with beta, either on hidden holds, hand and foot sequences or on gear placements. A "redpoint" refers to sending a route on lead but after at least one failed attempt. Rehearsing for a redpoint attempt may be done ground up on lead, lowering off the highpoint each time, by hangdogging, meaning hanging off the rope after a fall to work out the moves, or on top rope. A "pinkpoint" refers to redpointing a route but with the protection preplaced. In trad climbing, pinkpointing is often an intermediate objective before attempting a redpoint, placing gear on lead. In sport climbing, it is becoming more and more common for climbers to try their projects with the quickdraws pre-hung on the bolts, technically a pinkpoint. Sometimes in order to avoid a potential ground fall, the first bolt of a route is pre-clipped using a stickclip ("cheater stick"). Sometimes on a strenuous trad climb, a leader may place the first few pieces of awkward protection and then downclimb back to the ground to rest without weighting the rope to preserve their redpoint attempt, before blasting up with renewed energy.

These distinctions may sound quite convoluted and contrived to you, and you're right to think so. The only important rule to follow regarding style, is to always be honest about the way in which you climbed a route. It's then up to you to determine the personal significance, and to the climbing community to determine the collective significance of the ascent.

Etiquette

Etiquette refers to managing our behavior at the crag so as not to negatively impact the experience of other climbers and non-climbers. Proper etiquette can be summed up by two rules: leave no trace and be nice. Climber etiquette, like environmental impact, can be extremely important as it may play a critical role in influencing land managers in their decision to maintain access or to close an area to climbing altogether.

List of good practices and proper etiquette

Regarding ethics:
- Don't chip holds in the rock
- Leave established climbs as they are - don't add bolts or fixed gear without consulting the first ascensionists
- Avoid placing pitons which scar the rock, especially on established free climbs
- Don't place bolts unless you:
  1. Know what you're doing,
  2. Have permission from the landowner/manager, and
  3. Have the support of the local climbing community
- Don't bolt cracks
- Respect local ethics
- Respect the style of the first ascensionist

Regarding style:
- Climb however you like,
- Don't lie about it

INTRODUCTION

Regarding etiquette:
- Leave no trace, leave the crag cleaner than how you found it
- Remove chalk and tick marks even if they're not yours. To other climbers they make onsight climbing impossible. To non-climbers they're graffiti.
- Minimize chalk use, particularly on dark-colored stone
- Keep a low profile
- Climb in small groups
- If you bring your dog to the crag, tie them to a tree so they don't distract other belayers or step on ropes
- Keep noise down
- Despite the bad example set by certain professional climbers, try not to scream too too loud when you're working your project. Just because you're climbing a hard route shouldn't justify destroying the peace and tranquility of other climbers trying to enjoy a quiet afternoon at the crag.
- Never play music at the crag. The birds sing well enough.
- Keep drone use to a minimum if there are other climbers around. These whirligigs are loud, obnoxious and irritating for others. Besides, they may even be illegal.
- Be courteous and considerate to climbers, landowners, and other users
- Don't monopolize routes. If there are other parties waiting for the climb it's not the best time to hangdog.
- Park your car in the right place
- Make sure you have the right to be there
- Pay access fees when they exist

Thousands of tired, nerve-shaken, over-civilized people are beginning to find out that going to the mountains is going home; that wildness is a necessity; and that mountain parks and reservations are useful not only as fountains of timber and irrigating rivers, but as fountains of life.

-John Muir

Chapter 1 - Basic Equipment

In climbing we regularly entrust our lives to our partner and our equipment. We therefore must possess complete confidence in both in order to enjoy the sport. Climbing equipment is designed to be unquestionably strong, able to hold many times the forces generated in real life situations (especially in a top roping scenario). Thus, equipment that is in good condition and used properly doesn't fail. What is essential then is to know how to correctly operate the equipment, recognize the factors that cause wear and possess proper judgement in when to retire it. Unlike the climbing gym, there is no one else responsible for the equipment besides yourself.

The "Union Internationale des Associations d'Alpinisme" (UIAA) is an international climbing organisation that has become the gold standard for setting the safety norms and certification process of climbing equipment. They collaborate with the more general "Conformité Européenne" (CE) who essentially use the base UIAA standards for their certification (although in certain cases the UIAA certifications require additional tests making them stricter than CE). All climbing equipment should be certified by either the UIAA or CE. Look for the following symbols on your gear:

Although historically climbers often built and modified their own equipment to fit their needs, we now have the luxury of well-established manufactures of specialised climbing equipment with informed safety norms and a rigorous testing process. When you purchase climbing equipment, be sure to read the manual and follow any recommendations of the manufacturer. There are sometimes subtle differences in operation between models of similar pieces of equipment that would be impossible to sufficiently cover in this text.

Strength of climbing gear is usually measured as the number of Kilonewtons (kN) it can resist before breaking. A Newton (N) is a measure of force defined as that needed to accelerate one Kilogram of mass at the rate of 1m/s/s and a kN is simply 1000 N. Force and not weight is used because climbing situations involve falling masses (the climber), and a falling mass weighs more than a static one. Top rope climbing mostly resembles a static situation where, if the rope is always tight above the climber, the climber never "falls" (accelerating downwards before being caught by the rope), but instead simply weights the rope. In such a static situation, 1kN = ~100kg.

The climbing safety system known as the belay chain, (running from the climber's harness, the tie-in knot, the rope, to the belay anchor, back down the rope, belay device, to the belayer's harness) is designed to hold up to 15 kN of force, or ~1,500 kg, (25kN for the top belay anchor due to the pulley effect). This is around an order of magnitude greater than what is actually generated in a top rope situation. However, in lead climbing where the climber has time to accelerate during a fall, forces are increased significantly from a static situation. For a full explanation of forces in climbing see Chapter 4 on lead climbing.

BASIC EQUIPMENT

Weight		Static Force
lbs	kg	(kN)
100	45	0.44
125	57	0.56
150	68	0.67
175	80	0.78
200	91	0.89
220	100	0.98

Weight to force conversion table

Nylon material

Most textile climbing equipment including the harness, rope, cordelette (small diameter rope), and most slings are made from nylon. Nylon, a synthetic polymer based on polyamide, was first developed by the Dupont company in 1935 and quickly replaced the use of organic fibers such as hemp, manila and sisal. It is suitable for climbing applications thanks to its strength, elasticity, and abrasion-resistant properties.

Despite its advantages, nylon doesn't last forever as the fibers degrade over time, weakening as they dry out. Most manufacturers indicate the absolute lifespan of nylon climbing equipment as no more than 10 years from the date of manufacturing. If in use, most manufactures suggest a maximum lifespan of five years since first used. In reality, equipment should often be retired much sooner due to use-based wear.

Factors that damage nylon can be grouped into three categories: chemical wear, physical wear and environmental wear.

Chemical wear

Acids and other corrosive substances such as bleach are the worst enemy of nylon. Ensure that your equipment never comes in contact with such chemicals and retire immediately if it does. Be especially careful when throwing your gear into the trunk of your car. Dangerous corrosives (like leaking acid from an old car battery) could spell the end for your rope (and your life). Never write directly on your gear with permanent marker as tests have shown that this significantly weakens it. DEET, the active ingredient in bug spray also damages nylon so be sure to remove your harness before spraying yourself. Even the weak acidity of urine can help degrade your harness over time as does the salt residue of sweat, which accelerates drying and makes the nylon brittle. Wash salt and urine out with water to prevent long term damage.

Physical wear

Nylon equipment is most often worn out by physical factors. Since physical wear is inevitable and often progressive, it is essential to monitor the state of your gear before each use and to retire it when you have any reasonable doubt of its integrity.

Abrasion and friction can quickly wear out nylon. Sharp textured rock can cut through nylon gear if you're not careful. This is most probable when the nylon is under tension, and repeatedly abraded at the same spot. Such is the case of the rope running over a sharp rock during a rappel.

Nylon can also become severely damaged when it rubs against other nylon. The friction generated by nylon on nylon (or other textiles) can generate enough heat to burn through the gear. In most situations, a carabiner can serve as a connecting link between two nylon components (such as slings, cordelette or the rope), especially when one of the nylon components is moving. Even without moving components, (connecting two slings together,) nylon on nylon will significantly decrease the initial strength of the slings (see "connecting slings" in Chapter 3 for a more nuanced explanation) and should be avoided. The rope running through the harness tie-in points (which are reinforced to be abrasion resistant) will cause wear over the longer term that should be monitored. If any nylon gear shows any visible signs of wear (is cut, burnt, or abraded) or if it has experienced abnormally high shock, it should be retired.

BASIC EQUIPMENT

Nylon can be further degraded when small particles (like sand or dirt) are ground into its fibers. For this reason, equipment should be kept clean, and care should be taken to avoid stepping on it.

Environmental factors

UV light will damage nylon fibers. Equipment that has seen too much sunlight will be faded in colour and brittle and dry to the touch. Be especially careful of nylon gear that has been left outside such as permanent rappel anchors. If it looks damaged, cut if off and replace it with new material. Nylon slings left on a cliff face won't last for more than a season or two.

Nylon gear should not be exposed to extreme temperatures (over 60^0C or under -62^0C). Also, long term exposure to humid conditions will promote the growth of an ecosystem on your gear which could prove more serious than simply the stench.

Storage

Nylon gear should then be stored in a cool, dry environment, away from sunlight and heat sources, such as in a closet. It is a good idea to keep your rope in a rope bag to protect it from sharp objects in your pack, dangerous substances in your trunk and general dirt outside. Be sure to unpack all your gear after a day of climbing to let it dry before storing it. Never leave a wet rope in your pack.

It is a good practice to wash your gear once a year to prevent the dirt from grinding into the nylon fibers and accelerating damage. This can be done with warm water and a gentle soap in the bathtub. Be sure that there are no residues of harmful chemicals (such as bleach) in the tub before. Waiting for a rope to dry may take patience, but never resort to hanging it in direct sunlight or using artificial heat. Instead, flake it loosely in a cool, dry, well-ventilated place. Reflake it periodically to insure even drying. A simple house fan can be used to speed up the drying process.

Harness

Modern climbing harnesses are much more comfortable than the makeshift swami belts of the past or the old-school rope-tied-around-the-waist technique and help make falling reasonable and safe. They consist of a padded waist loop and two padded leg loops all connected by a central belay loop. The belay loop, rated to a minimum 15 kN, is the full-strength point where a carabiner attaches to the harness. Where the belay loop attaches to the waist and leg-loops are known as the two tie-in points and is where any nylon material (including the rope, personal tether, or slings) should be attached to the harness. Unlike the belay loop, the nylon of the harness tie-in points is protected with abrasion-resistant coating (often Kevlar) to prevent the nylon rope from sawing the nylon harness with the heat caused by friction. Furthermore, being tied into two points instead of one will help the climber remain upright in the event of a fall. The gear loops on the sides of the main waist loop are designed to hold gear you're not using and aren't weight-rated.

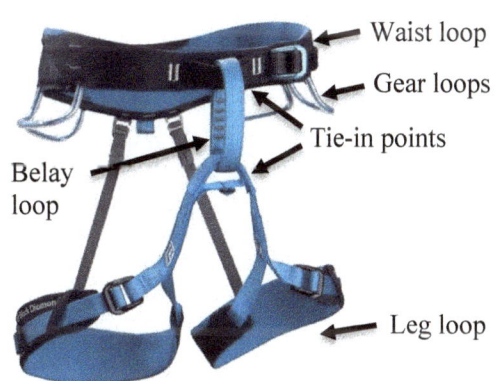

Standard harness

It is important to note that there are two main types of harness buckles: auto-locking buckles and the older double-back buckles (also called 3-pass buckles). Auto-locking buckles consist of two

BASIC EQUIPMENT

metal plates pressed against each other and are locked by simply pulling the sling tight. For the older double-back buckles, it is essential to pass the sling back a second time through the buckle to lock it off.

Auto-locking buckle

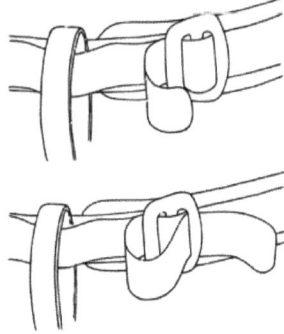
Double-back buckle

For either type, the sling should cover one side of the metal buckle which then resembles a "C" (closed), and not a full "O" (open).

A harness correctly worn should have no twists in any of the slings, should be worn above the hips and over clothing, and tightened down such that it is impossible to slip out of.

You should regularly inspect the state of your harness for signs of wear and retire it before the maximum 5-year in-use lifespan if there are visible signs of wear at the belay loop, tie-in points, waist, or leg loops or any of the important stitch points (denoted by a thread colour contrasting that of the harness). Climbers have died from harness failure, most notably, a world class alpinist whose belay loop snapped on an old harness that should have been replaced years earlier.

Rope

The climbing rope is undeniably the most important piece of equipment we have. What distinguishes a climbing rope from other ropes is its elasticity. Not only must it be strong, it also needs to elongate in order to absorb energy and decrease the impact force felt by the climber and the rest of the system during a fall. Older static ropes were plenty strong, but their lack of elasticity would result in huge forces generated by small falls. Although static and semi-static ropes are used in specific climbing scenarios (for anchor rigging, rappelling, fixing, hauling, etc.) the main climbing rope that catches a climber's fall must be dynamic (elastic).

The UIAA certifies 3 types of dynamic climbing ropes:

- Single ropes
- Double/half ropes
- Twin ropes

Single ropes are designed to be used as a single strand and are denoted by the number 1 inside a circle. Smaller diameter double (also called half) ropes are designed to be used in pairs but clipped alternately into protection. They are denoted by ½ inside a circle. Of even smaller diameter are twin ropes designed to be used in pairs, both ropes clipped into each and every piece of protection. They are denoted by two overlapping circles inside a larger circle. Note that some ropes might possess more than one such certification.

 Single rope

 Half rope

 Twin rope

BASIC EQUIPMENT

In nearly all climbing situations (with the exception of ice climbing, mountaineering and complex trad climbing), a single rope is desired. For a full explanation on the use of double and twin ropes, see Chapter 7 on traditional climbing.

Modern dynamic climbing ropes are what are called "Kernmantle". First introduced in 1953 by Edelrid, they became the norm in climbing in the early 1970's. Kernmantle ropes consist of two separate parts, the braided inner core (kern) designed to provide the majority of the rope's strength, and the tightly-woven outer sheath (or mantle) designed to protect the inner core from abrasion. Both the core and the sheath are made of nylon.

The white core is made of many strands twisted together, and the green sheath is woven around the core to protect it from abrasion

Ropes differ in their length, diameter, elasticity, strength, waterproofing (dry treatment), etc. To better understand rope properties and know which to buy, it is necessary to consider the UIAA drop test and corresponding certifications.

UIAA drop test

The UIAA drop test is a standardised test where the rope is stressed consecutively until breakage. Although severe and unrealistic, it provides a comprehensive analysis and conservative standards for the use of ropes in real-world climbing situations.

The drop test for single ropes involves attaching an 80kg mass to 2.8 meters of rope and raising it 2.5 meters above a metal lip, similar to a carabiner. The mass is dropped resulting in a "fall factor" of 1.78 (the total length of the fall divided by the length of rope) and done so repeatedly until it breaks. This is a very high-force situation since there is little rope to absorb the energy generated by the fall. For a rope to pass the test, it must survive a minimum of 5 falls. Furthermore, for the first fall, the peak impact force generated must not exceed 12 kN with a corresponding rope elongation less or equal to 40%. The static elongation, determined by weighting the rope with the 80kg mass, must not exceed 10%. All certified ropes possess values for a series of properties determined by the drop test which can be used to compare ropes. These are:

- Peak impact force (first fall)
- Dynamic elongation (first fall)
- Static elongation
- Number of falls held

Although any UIAA-certified single rope is suitable for both top roping and lead climbing, it is important to review the specs in order to choose a rope best suited to the situation you intend on using it in.

The first two values, peak impact force and dynamic elongation are intimately related. A more dynamic rope with a larger dynamic elongation will result in a smaller impact force (as the rope stretch absorbs energy). However, a more dynamic rope is generally less durable since repeated stretching wears the rope. For top roping, since fall forces are small, it is more important to have a rope with less elongation. Remember that 10% static elongation of a 60m rope (the beginning of a 30m climb) means that when the climber weights the rope the rope will elongate 6m (assuming no friction)! For lead climbing, a more dynamic rope with greater elongation and a lower peak impact force will make a fall smoother and more comfortable as well as decrease the force felt by the protection point (bolt

BASIC EQUIPMENT

or trad gear). Trad climbing, when the gear placements are not always as strong as you'd like, is made safer by using a more dynamic rope. However, there is a trade-off as more elongation means falling further and potentially hitting a ledge or bulge. Finally, the number of falls held indicates overall rope durability and the ability of the rope to quickly recuperate its dynamic properties after a fall.

A common misconception is that the value for the number of falls held corresponds with the number of falls the rope can hold in the real world before it should be retired. If not already clear, I must stress that the UIAA drop test conditions are dramatically more severe than a real-world fall. First, the fall situation (high fall factor) is close to the worst possible fall, generating high forces. Also, in the real world the catch (how a fall is arrested) is more dynamic due several non-negligible factors excluded from in the test conditions. Things such as knots tightening, the belayer being pulled upwards, some rope slipping through the belay device, the ability of the body to flex and flail, will all significantly absorb energy and reduce the real peak impact force. Perhaps the most unrealistic aspect of the drop test is that falls are consecutive without giving the rope time to recover. After the first fall, the rope stretches but never regains its full elasticity before the subsequent fall and becomes more and more static, increasing the impact force with each fall. In the real world the rope will have time to recover. Finally, each repeated fall loads the rope over the metal edge at exactly the same spot, also highly improbable in the real world.

<u>What rope to buy</u>

Single ropes range in diameter from about 9mm to 11mm although diameters have been decreasing in recent years to make ropes lighter. However, thinner ropes, as well as being more expensive, are less durable and won't last as long. For top roping, since weight is not an issue, it is best to use a thick and durable rope, from 9.8-10.3mm. Note that ropes fatter than 10.3mm won't fit into certain new belay devices such as the Petzl Grigri. Sport climbing may warrant a thinner rope, as those few grams may be the difference between sending your project or not. Trad climbers should choose a rope that decreases the peak impact force.

The standard rope length in North America for both top roping and lead climbing is 60m (although this has been increasing over time from 50m in the 1970's to 60m, to even 70m for some new sport climbing sites). A 60m rope permits climbs up to 30m.

Some ropes have a core and/or sheath that is dry treated, making it waterproof. While this is essential for ice climbing and alpinism, this dry treatment will quickly wear off from abrasion when climbing textured rock and so is a waste of money for a rope used primarily for rock climbing. However, tests have shown that a rope loses 30-50% of its strength when wet as well as becoming less abrasion resistant, so a good general rule is to refrain from climbing on a wet rope.

<u>When to retire a rope</u>

Always take a few minutes to flake your rope and inspect the integrity of its sheath before the first climb of the day. This involves running the length of the rope through your hand to untangle any knots and at the same time looking for any sheath damage. You should also periodically inspect the rope thoroughly to assess the integrity of the sheath and core. Damage to the sheath can be assessed visually but core damage must be evaluated by feel. You should retire a rope if the sheath is cut and the core is visible, if the sheath is excessively fuzzy or worn, or if the core has sections that are soft, flat or abnormal to the touch, or if you are able to bend the rope without resistance such that it completely folds on itself. Even if a rope seems in good condition, retire it if it has caught an extremely severe fall or after a maximum of five years of use.

BASIC EQUIPMENT

A damaged core

<u>Coiling a rope</u>

There are two common ways to coil a rope after use, a butterfly coil or a mountaineer's coil.

<u>Butterfly coil</u>

Whereas the mountaineer's coil is commonly used in alpine situations where the climber may need to climb with part of the rope coiled over their shoulder, the butterfly coil is the standard coil in a cragging context. Start by coiling the rope with equal-length loops on each side of your neck. Move the coil onto your forearm, then with the final few meters of rope, wrap the coil several times from the bottom up. Pass a bight of rope through the eye of the coil and finish with a girth hitch.

Butterfly coil

To make a butterfly coil that can be worn as a backpack, start by finding the middle of the rope and wrap both strands simultaneously to make

23

BASIC EQUIPMENT

the main coil. Finish by pulling both ends through the final girth hitch. The two strands can then be used to wrap your shoulders and waist.

A butterfly coil worn as backpack

The backpack can be tied off around the waist with a strop bend (also known as a reef or square knot).

Strop bend

Mountaineer's coil

The mountaineer's coil can easily be worn over the shoulder and is often used by mountaineers to shorten the rope.

Mountaineer's coil

To use the rope, make sure to uncoil one loop at a time to prevent the rope becoming twisted.

Slings, webbing and runners

Used to build belay anchors, extend protection and in many other applications, slings are an essential piece of equipment for all types of outdoor climbing. When it is a single strand cut in bulk it is sometimes called webbing, whereas when it is sewn or tied in a loop it can be called a runner.

BASIC EQUIPMENT

One inch (25mm) nylon webbing, either flat or tubular, is the cheap option. You can buy it by the meter and cut it yourself and melt the ends with a flame (or stove element). Both Mil-spec and Climb-spec (military or climbing grade) are acceptable. Since webbing is often most useful as a loop, the two ends can be tied together with a water knot, (see Chapter 3, A note on slings).

Tensile vs. loop strength

Tensile strength refers to the resistance of a single strand of webbing whereas loop strength is the strength of the loop, or two strands. Therefore, loop strength should be twice the tensile strength minus the reduction in strength caused by the knot, or ~1.2x the tensile strength given 60% knot efficiency.

The strength of tubular webbing is generally denoted by the number of stitched stripes running lengthwise along it.

	Tensile strength	Loop strength
1 stripe	5 kN	6kN
2 stripes	10 kN	12kN
3 stripes	15 kN	18kN
4 stripes	20 kN	24kN

Tensile and loop strength of nylon tubular webbing

Two-stripe nylon tubular webbing

Two or three-stripped webbing is common. One-stripe is not strong enough and four-stripe is overkill. Always check the specifications and kN rating of the webbing you buy as there may be some variability between companies. Tensile strength should be at least 10kN.

Pre-sewn runners

Pre-sewn loops of 18mm diameter nylon slings are common. The sewn connection is less bulky and stronger than a hand-tied knot. The UIAA requires sewn slings (runners) to resist a minimum of 22kN (loop strength). Runners come in three standard lengths:

- 60cm (shoulder sling)
- 120cm (double shoulder sling)
- 240cm (quadruple shoulder sling)

These lengths are often colour-coded, where 60cm is yellow, 120 cm is blue and 240cm is grey.

Dyneema, Spectra and Dynex

Essentially three commercial names for the same material, this high molecular-weight polyethylene has a higher strength-weight ratio than steel. For simplicity's sake, I'll refer to all of these materials as Dyneema. Slings made of Dyneema are less bulky, lighter and more abrasion and cut-resistant than nylon slings. The downside is that they have a lower melting point than nylon, are too slippery to tie together with knots, and are almost twice the price. Furthermore, Dyneema is an extremely static material compared to the slight elasticity inherent in nylon. Depending on the situation, either nylon or Dyneema slings may be desirable.

BASIC EQUIPMENT

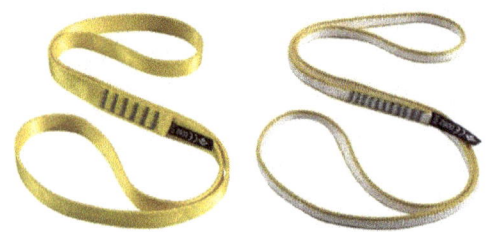

Two Black Diamond 60cm shoulder slings, the first nylon, the second Dynex.

Cordelette

Cordelette, small diameter usually nylon cord, is used when tied in a loop to rig anchors, sling protection and tie friction hitches. It comes in a variety of diameters from 4mm to 8mm.

Diameter	Tensile strength
4mm	3.2kN
5mm	5.0kN
6mm	7.2kN
7mm	9.9kN
8mm	12.8kN

Tensile strength of nylon cordelette

To be strong enough to be used as a single loop it should be minimum 7mm in diameter. This is because 7mm cordelette tied in a loop provides ~13.9 kN of resistance (9.9 x 2 x 70% knot efficiency), almost enough to be considered full strength in the belay chain (15kN). However, sometimes 6mm cordelette is preferred to tie a prusik on smaller diameter ropes, (see Chapter 3, rappelling).

Personal tether

A personal tether, also known as a personal anchoring system (PAS), is a short piece of dynamic rope tied to the harness tie-in points which can be used to clip directly into a belay anchor or to extend a rappel device. Older climbers may argue that the climbing rope itself should be used to tie in directly to a belay anchor in multi-pitch climbing, but it is undeniable that the use of a personal tether facilitates safer practices in a number of other situations including top rope rigging and multi-pitch rappelling. Although you may see some climbers using a static nylon sling as a personal tether, (or worse a dyneema daisy chain made for aid-climbing,) a *dynamic* tether is far safer when clipping oneself in directly to a belay anchor. DMM tests have shown that a short fall onto a belay anchor, where there is no dynamic component in the system, can generate enough force to cause equipment failure. Using a dynamic personal tether ensures that there is always a component in the system that can absorb energy in the case of a slip at the belay anchor. Even so, when clipped in directly to an anchor with your tether, be sure to remain low such that the tether has little to no slack in it. A slip that results in shock loading your tether would be at best extremely uncomfortable. A personal tether can be made DIY with ~2.5m of any single-rated dynamic climbing rope or bought pre-made such as the Beal Dynaclip. To attach a pre-made personal tether to your harness, girth hitch it either through the two tie-in-points or through the belay loop (although the belay loop will wear faster from abrasion).

Beal Dynaclip dynamic personal tether girth hitched through the harness tie-in points

BASIC EQUIPMENT

To make your own personal tether, tie into the (2.5m) rope with a figure 8 follow-through, tie a figure-of-8 on a bight at the other end and an alpine butterfly in the middle, (see Chapter 2, knots and hitches).

Personal tether made from 2.5m of climbing rope

Helmet

Wearing a helmet is always a good idea when climbing outdoors. Since its primary purpose is to protect you from the downward impact of rock fall, it is of equal or greater importance that the belayer wears a helmet as well.

A helmet is critical in situations where there is increased risk of rock fall:

- areas with loose rock (most areas)
- if there are hikers or other climbers above that may dislodge rocks
- if the cliff is higher than a single pitch

The helmet should be intended for rock climbing and certified as such.

Carabiners

Carabiners are metal clips used primarily to connect various links in the anchor or belay chain. Carabiners are made from an alloy of aluminum and zinc. Whereas aluminum is extremely lightweight, the addition of zinc adds strength. Although some carabiners are made of steel, they are significantly heavier and intended for industrial applications instead of recreational climbing.

Shapes

Carabiners come in a variety of forms. The basic design is an oval with an opening on one side bridged by a mechanical spring-loaded gate.

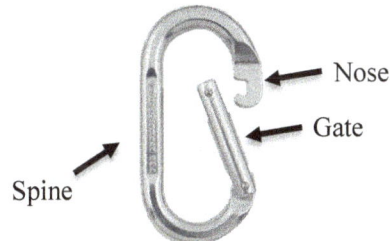

The parts of a basic carabiner

Although ovals are still useful in certain situations because of their symmetry (racking for example), more compact asymmetrical D-shaped carabiners have become the standard. This is because their asymmetrical shape directs the load onto their spine, making it the strongest design. Pear-shaped carabiners have one small end and one wide end which can be useful in a variety of scenarios, the most common being for rappelling.

Oval, D- and pear-shaped carabiners

BASIC EQUIPMENT

Gates

The weakest part of a carabiner is its gate. Carabiners may have a straight solid gate, a bent solid gate or a wire gate.

Straight gate   *Bent gate*   *Wire gate*

- Solid gates are the standard and original gate type.
- Curved solid gates facilitate easy clipping with one hand. This makes them suitable for the rope end of a quickdraw (sport climbing).
- Wire gate carabiners may be more expensive but are lighter and safer than solid gates. Although they look flimsy, they actually increase the strength of the carabiner by reducing something called gate flutter. During a fall, the rope running through the carabiner causes the gate to vibrate, quickly fluttering open and shut. Since the amplitude of the flutter is proportional to the mass of the gate, the lighter wire gate actually helps to keep the gate shut during a fall. Furthermore, wire gates don't freeze shut like solid gates when winter climbing and will have a wider opening making them easier to handle with gloves on.

The place where the gate attaches to the nose is critical, responsible for the difference in closed vs. open-gate strength (a difference of about 10kN or 1000kg). The standard mechanism is a pin and notch. The newer notchless key-lock mechanism is superior as it handles more easily without getting snagged on your harness gear loops.

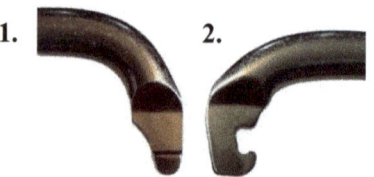

The noses of a 1. key-lock and 2. pin-and-notch carabiner

Locking carabiners

A locking mechanism on the gate prevents it from accidently opening and is thus a must for all critical junctions. Any time the entire belay chain is dependent on a single carabiner, it must be a locking one. Two main types of locking mechanisms exist. The most common is the screw-gate locking carabiner which is locked by screwing a collar down the gate.

Screw-gate carabiner

Always double check screw-gate carabiners to confirm they're locked (both visually and by pinching the gate). For those who have the tendency to forget such things, there exist spring-loaded auto-locking carabiners. However, fool-proof isn't always safer as it means losing the habit of double-checking yourself.

Three different spring-loaded auto-locking carabiners

BASIC EQUIPMENT

Strength

The UIAA requires all carabiners to resist a minimum force in 3 different situations. These are:

- closed gate strength in its major axis
- closed gate strength in its minor axis
- open gate strength in its major axis

All carabiners will have this information stamped on their spine.

This carabiner is rated to hold 20kN in its major axis, 7kN in its minor axis, and 8kN in its major axis with the gate open.

UIAA carabiner requirements:

	Major axis	Minor axis	Gate open
Oval	18kN	7kN	5kN
D-shaped	20kN	7kN	7kN
Locking	20kN	7kN	6kN

UIAA requirements for oval, D-shaped and locking carabiners

Note that a carabiner loses roughly 2/3 of its strength when it is loaded in its minor axis or loaded with the gate open. Furthermore, carabiners are designed to be loaded in only one axis. A carabiner loaded tri-axially (in 3 axes at once) will be significantly weakened. Make sure to keep carabiners loaded only along their major axis.

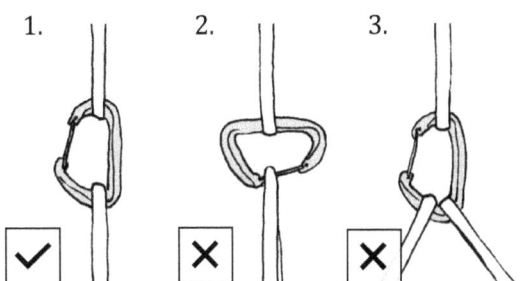

A carabiner loaded in its 1. major axis, 2. minor axis (cross loaded) and 3. tri-axially loaded

When a carabiner is loaded in a levered position, pressed up against a rock edge or angled in a bolt for example, its strength will be vastly reduced. It is hard to make generalisations about the strength of levered carabiners since a slight shift in the position of the fulcrum will dramatically change the forces experienced by the carabiner. However, some tests have shown failure at as little as 2.5kN when the carabiner was loaded with a severe lever.

Beware of the dreaded nose clip. A carabiner in this orientation can snap under very low forces.

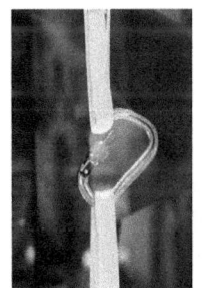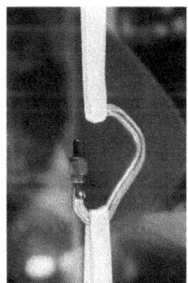

A locking carabiner nose clipped. In this Black Diamond test, the carabiner failed at only 5.2 kN.

When to retire a carabiner

Metal gear doesn't have a fixed life span like nylon equipment and may last for a long time if used minimally. Normal wear includes that from the friction of the rope running through it and damage due to metal on metal such as the carabiner clipped to a bolt hanger. The heat generated by the friction

BASIC EQUIPMENT

of the rope running through the carabiner will eventually wear away the metal. Retire a carabiner when it has lost 10% of its initial diameter.

This carabiner has become worn from repeated rappelling and should be retired.

Retire if there are sharp metal grooves cut into it. Not only has it become weakened, but the metal burs on the carabiner could subsequently damage the climbing rope as it runs through it. Be sure that the carabiner's gate is functioning properly and closes completely. If the gate is sticky or squeaky, first wash the carabiner in warm soapy water, dry it, then lubricate the hinge. Be sure to wipe off any excess lubricant to avoid getting residue on nylon slings or ropes. If a carabiner is dropped, the impact may cause micro cracks in the metal and compromise its integrity. Although tests on this are contradictory and inconclusive, manufacturers recommend retiring a carabiner if it is dropped from more than 3m onto a hard surface.

Quicklinks

Quicklinks are essentially cheaper, more durable locking carabiners. They aren't used in most applications because they are heavy and tedious to operate but are useful for leaving behind without regret. Bolt anchors are sometimes equipped with these to clip into and pass the rope through for rappels to protect the anchor bolts or bolt hangers from wear. A quicklink can be easily and cheaply replaced whereas a bolt cannot. Keeping one or two on your harness is a good idea for when you need to leave some gear behind (bailing off a route, replacing old rappel or anchor gear, etc.). Use quicklinks that have a force rating in kN, certified by CE or UIAA, and not one with a weight rating in lbs bought from a hardware store. The UIAA requires quicklinks to hold a minimum of 25kN in its major axis and 10kN in its minor axis (cross loaded).

A quicklink

Belay devices

A belay device is designed to create a sharp bend in the rope to generate enough friction for the belayer to easily hold the climber's weight. The most common belay devices fall into one of two main categories:

1. Traditional belay tubes
2. Assisted-braking devices

Traditional belay tubes

Belay tubes are often simply referred to as ATCs because of an early Black Diamond model of the same name. Like belay plates which they largely replaced, they consist simply of one or two slots in either a metal plate or tube in which to pinch the rope through, and a cable to clip a carabiner to.

Belay plate   *Belay tube*

Most models will have two adjacent slots to make rappelling possible as well as belaying. Since rappelling is not practised indoors, gym climbers may opt to use a single slot device such as the ATC sport. Sometimes teeth are added to the side where the brake end of the rope sits which creates more friction making it easier to arrest a fall.

BASIC EQUIPMENT

Although not necessary, a toothed device like the ATC XP is often preferred over the original toothless ATC. Finally, an additional metal loop may be found on one side of the device, such as the ATC Guide which is used in multi-pitch climbing to belay from above, (see Chapter 5 on multi-pitch climbing).

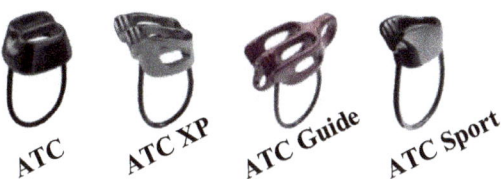

A variety of traditional tube belay devices from Black Diamond

Belaying with a traditional tube or plate device, there are two basic positions one can hold the brake end of the rope. Holding the brake end of the rope in an open position, higher than the device such that the two strands are parallel, provides little-to-no friction and makes it near to impossible to hold the climber. However, holding the brake end of the rope in a blocked position, below the device, generates enough friction to easily hold the climber. This happens as the belay device pinches the rope against the carabiner creating a sharp bend and generating friction.

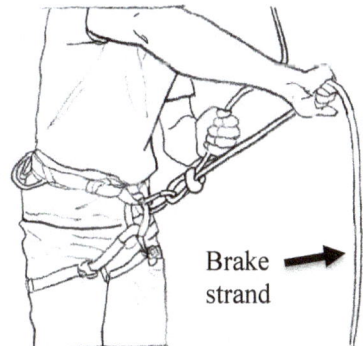

The open position, holding the brake strand higher than the belay device, generates next to no friction

The blocked position, holding the brake strand lower than the belay device generates sufficient friction to hold a fall

Assisted-braking belay devices

Unlike traditional belay tubes, assisted-braking belay devices lock off automatically during a fall and help to hold the climber's weight. This is done either by a mechanical camming mechanism that physically pinches the rope (active), or by the geometry of the device which causes it to rotate and pinch the rope against the belay carabiner (passive).

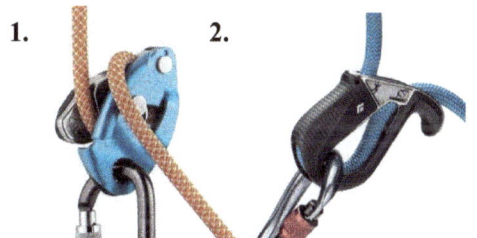

1. The Petzl Grigri, a common camming assisted-braking device
2. The Black Diamond ATC Pilot, a common geometry assisted-braking belay device

If ever the belayer loses control of the brake end of the rope because they slip on uneven belay terrain, are hit by rock fall, stung by a bee, etc., using an assisted-braking belay device may be what prevents the climber from hitting the ground. For this reason, such devices are a valuable tool for outdoor climbing.

BASIC EQUIPMENT

Assisted-braking belay devices are however not suited to all situations. Because of the more abrupt braking action, these devices tend to increase the amount of force generated during a leader fall and are therefore unsuitable for traditional climbing when the protection points are rarely as strong as bolts. Also, since most assisted-braking devices only hold a single strand of rope, they can't be used for rappelling.

Although assisted-braking devices have the potential to increase safety in most situations, like any belay device, they only work effectively when used correctly, according to the manufacturer's recommendations. The often-increased likelihood of user-error due to a false sense of security is particularly unfortunate. Using idiot-proof belay devices tends to turn belayers into idiots. There is no such thing as a magic belay device. In the end, the device is only as safe as the belayer.

Any of the above belay devices should be retired when there are visible signs of wear, if it has become sharpened from rope friction, or, like a carabiner, it is dropped onto a hard surface from higher than 3m.

Bolts

Permanent steel bolts drilled into the rock often serve as anchor points for top rope belay anchors, as well as intermediate protection points on sport climbs. Bolted top anchors are desirable for high-traffic areas as they lessen the environmental impact of the repeated use of trees. Bolts have been placed by climbers for the last 50 years and have become widespread with the advent of sport climbing 35 years ago. However, many of these older bolts placed before the 2000s may no longer be safe. Although climbing associations (such as the FQME in Québec) invest much of their energies into replacing old bolts and monitoring the state new ones, it is still the responsibility of the climber to assess each and every bolt they clip into. Before we learn to identify old and bad bolts, let's first become familiar with good bolts. There are two types of modern bolts:

1. Expansion bolts with bolt hangers and
2. Glue in bolts.

1. Expansion bolt & bolt hanger   *2. Glue-in bolt*

Both made of (usually stainless) steel, expansion bolts expand into the drilled bolt hole as they are pounded whereas glue-in bolts are sealed into the rock with epoxy. Note that expansion bolts may have either a nut to tighten the hanger onto the bolt, or the bolt head may itself be hexagonal and tighten onto the hanger. The UIAA requires all bolts to resist a downward and outward force of 25 and 20KN, (~2,500 & 2,000 kg of static weight).

<u>Bolt assessment</u>

In most regions, especially those that see high traffic, most bolts are new and in good condition. However, it isn't rare to sometimes encounter older bolts that may or may not be safe. In order to assess the quality of older bolts it is useful to know a little about the history of climbing bolts.

In the 1960s and 70s, bolts were placed mainly by hand and on the lead. Climbers would adapt whatever equipment they could get a hold of and sometimes make their own from scrap metal. This culture of do-it-yourself engineering enabled climbing, a fringe activity, to progress rapidly and thrive throughout its golden age, but is also responsible for an array of old, sometimes poorly placed, corroded hardware. The most popular bolt from this era was a ¼ inch compression bolt named the Rawl drive, designed by the Rawl company for construction and industrial applications.

Rawl drive ¼ inch compression bolt

A compression bolt has a split shaft that is slightly wider than the diameter of the bolt hole and so deforms as it is pounded in. This works well when set in hard rock types like granite and indeed the shear strength of a new Rawl drive bolt is ~9KN (strong but still far less than the 25KN UIAA requirement). However, the real danger is when these are placed in softer rock types like sandstone. Here, although the shear strength may still be considerable, the outward pullout strength can be extremely variable where some can be easily yanked out of the rock with a sharp pull. Similarly, Nail and sleeve Star Dryvins, recognizable by the characteristic star stamped on the bolt head, may have insufficient pull-out strength when placed in soft rock types.

Star Dryvin (nail and sleeve) bolt

Both Rawl drives and Star Dryvins may be dangerous for a several further reasons. The ¼ inch diameter of these bolts is already questionably small, but worse is that they came in a variety of lengths, the smallest being only ¾ inch, and once in the rock, there is no way of knowing how long they are. Furthermore, any of these bolts, placed over 30 years ago are likely heavily rusted making them more dangerous still. For these reasons, all ¼ inch bolts should be avoided entirely. They can easily be identified due to their button head (Rawl Drive), star stamp (Star Dryvins), or small diameter threaded bolt stem. They will almost always be rusty as well.

Two old ¼ inch bolts, a buttonhead and a star dryvin

Although the late 80s saw buttonheads getting wider with a standard diameter of 5/16-inch, it wasn't until the 1990s that 3/8-inch diameter became the norm. Modern expansion and glue-in bolts should be 3/8-inch when set in hard rock like granite, and ½-inch when set in soft rock like sandstone.

Another problem with 1970s era bolts is the bolt hanger. The most common hanger was the SMC, whose name is clearly stamped on it. There were two series of hangers, the first which are very dangerous, the second which may be acceptable. The first series, the "SMC death hangers" has "SMC" stamped horizontally onto the hanger, whereas the slightly newer and thicker diameter hangers have SMC stamped vertically on them.

BASIC EQUIPMENT

1. SMC death hanger on an old rusty ¼ inch threaded Rawl drive - DANGEROUS
2. SMC vertical hanger on a 5/16-inch buttonhead – BETTER, but still not great

Another dangerous but common bolt hanger from the 1970s is the Leeper hanger. It is easily recognizable by its unique shape. After 9,000 of these Colorado-made hangers were put up, they were recalled due to stress corrosion problems.

Leeper bolt hanger on a buttonhead

Finally, it's also not uncommon to come across homemade bolt hangers. These may be of varying quality. Don't trust them.

A homemade bolt hanger
Photo: safeclimbing.org

To assess the quality of a bolt, one must consider the bolt diameter and type, the bolt hanger, the state of the hardware and the rock itself. Here is a list of things to consider when assessing a bolt:

- The rock must be solid, not part of a detached flake or block
- The bolt should never be placed closer than 15cm to a crack or arête
- Be sure that there are no spiderweb-like fractures emanating from the bolt hole (common for compression bolts)
- Bolts should be at least 3/8-inches in diameter
- Beware of buttonheads and Star Dryvins
- Beware of the SMC death hanger, Leeper hanger, or any funky homemade hanger
- Rusted or corroded bolts should be treated with caution
- Don't trust a bolt if it moves inside the bolt hole
- If the bolt hanger spins on the bolt, treat it with caution
- For glue-in bolts, the actual hole in the rock shouldn't be visible, as it should be filled completely with glue

> *Perhaps the crescent moon smiles in doubt at being told that it is a fragment awaiting perfection.*
>
> -Rabindranath Tagore

Chapter 2 – Knots and hitches

Knots and hitches allow us to adapt the rope for many specific purposes. The difference between a knot and a hitch is that a knot will hold its integrity regardless of whether it is fixed to something else, whereas a hitch, always tied around another object, relies on that object to hold. Any time a knot (or hitch) is tied into a strand of rope, the initial strength of that rope is reduced at the point of the knot. If enough force is applied until breakage, the rope will always fail at its weakest point, the knot. For a knot to function optimally and retain the highest residual strength, it must be dressed correctly, snugged down, and loaded in the intended manner.

In this chapter, all the basic knots and hitches are presented that should be mastered by all top rope, sport, and trad climbers. More advanced knots will be presented in later chapters when they become relevant.

Figure-of-8 on a bight

Figure-of-8 on a bight

Uses: To create a fixed loop of rope to clip a carabiner to.
Residual strength: ~80%
Notes: It is identical to the figure 8 follow-through but tied on two strands simultaneously. Minimum tail length is 10x the diameter of the rope (10cm for a standard climbing rope). Either or both strands can be loaded. Never load both strands at 180°.

Never load both strands of a figure-of-8 knot at 180°

Steps

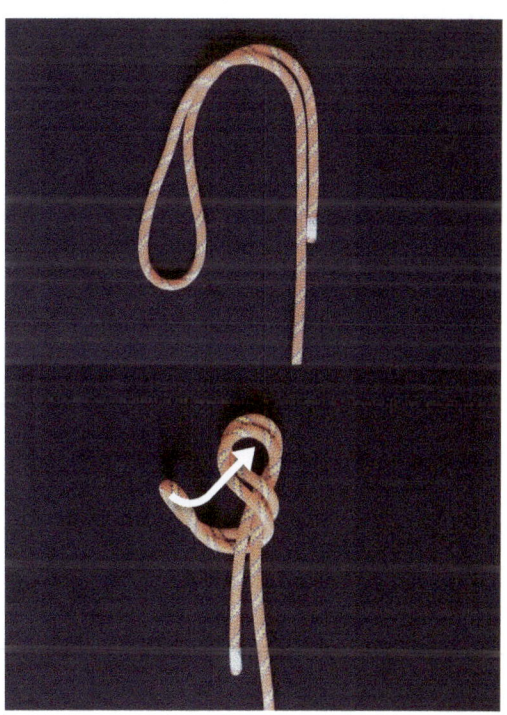

KNOTS AND HITCHES

Alpine butterfly

Alpine butterfly

Uses: Like a figure-of-8 on a bight, it serves to create a fixed loop of rope to clip a carabiner to. The difference is that the two strands are to be loaded in opposite directions at 180^0.
Residual strength: ~60%
Notes: Not to be tied near the rope's end.

Steps

KNOTS AND HITCHES

Clove hitch

Clove hitch

Uses: To securely attach the rope to a carabiner. This hitch works best on a pear-shaped carabiner. Unlike a figure-of-8 on a bight, it can be easily adjusted to shorten or lengthen the rope without having to undo it from the carabiner.
Residual strength: 60-65%
Notes: Can slip under extreme forces (factor 2 fall,) or if not set correctly. Do not tie near the end of the rope. Tighten by pulling each strand one at a time until snug on the carabiner. To optimize the strength of the carabiner, the load strand should be the one closer to the carabiner's spine.

Steps

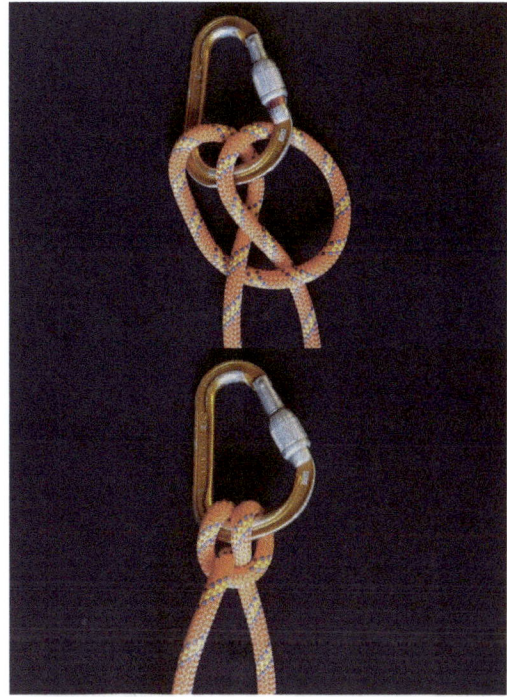

Stopper knot

Stopper knot

Uses: Tied in the end of the rope(s) when rappelling, or when belaying a leader on a single-pitch route. If the rope is too short, the stopper knot will block in the belay device.
Residual strength: N/A
Notes: Minimum tail length is 10x the diameter of the rope (10cm for a standard climbing rope).

37

KNOTS AND HITCHES

Steps

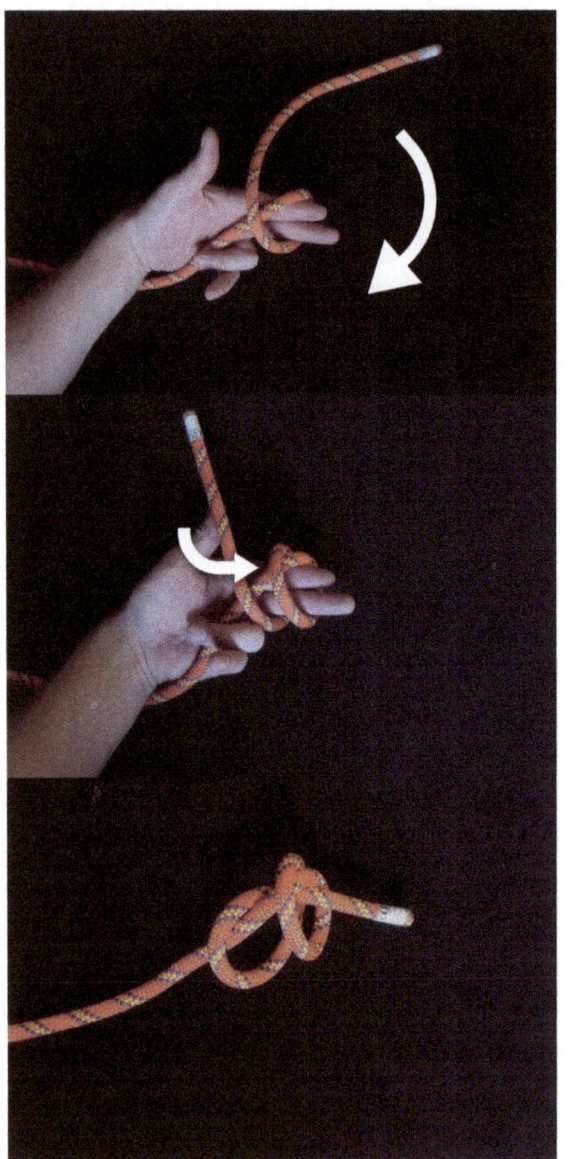

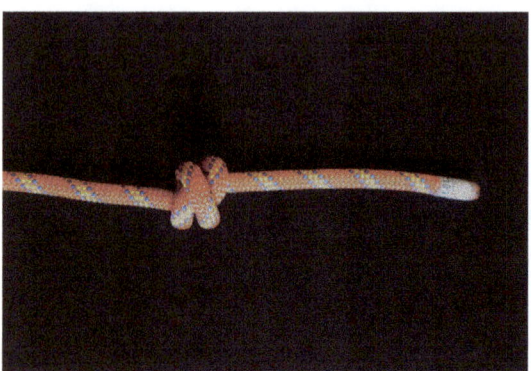

Double fisherman's bend

Double fisherman's

Essentially two stopper knots tied to block against each other.
Uses: to join two ropes together, either for a two-rope rappel, or to make a loop of cordelette
Residual strength: 65-70%
Notes: To be correctly dressed, the two ropes should wrap in opposite directions which will result in the two final "X"s nested against each other on the same side of the knot. If this is not the case, untie one of the two ropes and wrap in the other direction. Minimum tail length is 10x the diameter of the rope, (or slightly shorter when the knot is snug).

KNOTS AND HITCHES

Steps

Prusik hitch

Three-wrap prusik hitch

Uses: Tied around the thicker climbing rope, it creates enough friction to hold the main rope when weighted but can slide along it when unweighted. It is often used as a rappel back up (third hand), for moving on a fixed line and in rescue situations.
Residual strength: 65-70% (in cordelette)
Notes: Friction is increased by adding more wraps or by increasing the difference between diameters of the two ropes, (using a smaller-diameter cordelette or larger-diameter main line). Make sure the prusik is well set before you trust it.

Steps

KNOTS AND HITCHES

Uses: The simplest way to attach a loop of rope, cordelette or webbing around a fixed point (like a tree or harness tie-in points)
Residual strength: 65-70%
Notes: Make sure the hitch is positioned so that it does not strangle the strands, creating an unnecessarily sharp bend in the rope.

A correctly and poorly positioned girth hitch. Strangling the sling decreases its strength and will wear it prematurely.

Girth hitch

Girth hitch

> All the birds have flown up and gone;
> A lonely cloud floats leisurely by.
> We never tire of looking at each other –
> Only the mountain and I.
>
> -Li Po

Chapter 3 – Top rope

Top rope (also known as a sling-shot belay) refers to an anchor configuration where the rope runs from the climber, through the belay anchor at the top of the route, and back down to the belayer. In this way, the climber is always well-protected since they are always situated beneath the top belay anchor. If the rope is kept mostly taught, then the consequence of a fall will only ever be minimal. Top roping is therefore the best low-risk system to enjoy outdoor climbing.

In a climbing gym, the rope already runs through a permanent top rope belay anchor and both strands are hanging by the ground, ready for the climber and belayer to attach themselves. In an outdoor context, the team may arrive at the cliff from the top or the bottom, must safely access the cliff edge, choose anchor points, construct a belay anchor, then descend to the ground by either hiking or rappelling before they find themselves at the starting point of an indoor climb.

Scouting the anchor position

For a cliff to be suitable for top rope climbing, it must meet three basic criteria: it must be shorter than 30m (half the length of a standard rope), it must have access to the top by a walk-around trail, and it must provide suitable anchors (usually bolts or trees). Guidebooks will normally indicate whether a site is suited to top roping or not. Some sites may require a long hike and significant bushwhacking to reach cliff edge, others may involve a 3-minute walk. Before travelling to a crag, first do your research.

To efficiently scout a top rope anchor position, the first step is to find the route you want to climb. If arriving from the bottom, try to scout the ideal anchor position from the ground, taking note of prominent landmarks such as trees or rock features both at the top and bottom of the cliff. If the desired anchor position possesses no distinguishing feature, instead look for the closest landmark, for example, ~10m left of the large tree. It is often best that one person hikes around to the top while the other remains on the ground to aid their partner locate a suitable anchor location. This is also important in case another party arrives with the intention of leading the same route. Whoever is there first has priority.

Installing and using a fixed rope

Often it may be necessary to install and attach oneself to a fixed rope in order to safely approach cliff edge and set up a belay anchor. Many unfortunate accidents could be prevented by being more cautious here. If you don't have the necessary equipment to install a fixed rope, you are more likely to take unnecessary risks while setting up your belay anchor. Unless you know the site, always carry ~20-30m of static rope (9-11mm) for this purpose. Although a strand of dynamic climbing rope is also acceptable, a static rope can double for rigging a belay anchor on trees, explained later in this chapter, and is therefore the best choice.

A fixed rope is called such simply because one end is fixed to an anchor, meaning that unlike a top rope, it doesn't move. Instead, you move along the fixed rope with the use of a friction hitch or mechanical belay device. To set up a fixed rope, begin by locating solid anchor points well back from the dangerous terrain. This is often a big, solid tree, well back in the forest, or at times a set of bolts, placed for this purpose.

Tree anchor

Make sure the tree is alive, well-rooted, and larger than 40cm in diameter at its base. Attach the rope using a rethreaded figure-of-8 (figure 8 follow-through). Tie a figure 8, wrap the tree close to its base, then rethread the knot.

A rope fixed to a tree

Two-bolt anchor

With the exception of a giant tree, it is always preferable to use two independent anchor points in the case that one fails. Although a single bolt is almost certainly sufficiently strong, the standard is to always use a minimum of two in conjunction to provide this redundancy. Consequently, bolts are always placed in pairs. Below is a standard 2-bolt set-up.

→ **Expansion bolt**

→ **Bolt hanger**

→ **Quicklink**

→ **Rappel ring**

A standard 2-bolt set-up

There are several acceptable ways to fix a rope to two bolts. Here I prioritize simple setups that use only minimal gear. I suggest fixing the rope to the first bolt with a figure 8 follow-through, then to the second with an alpine butterfly. Note that if the bolts have quicklinks, rap rings, chains or are glue-in bolts (such as in the photo below), you can simply pass your rope directly through it. If the anchors are expansion bolts with hangers and without any other hardware, then you'll need to use carabiners to protect your rope from the sharp metal. **Never pass a rope or sling directly through a bolt hanger.**

← **Glue-in bolt**

← **Figure 8 follow-through**

← **Alpine butterfly**

A rope fixed to two glue-in bolts with a figure 8 follow-through and alpine butterfly

Alternatively, the double-loop figure-of-8 on a bight provides a better way to fix the rope such that both anchor points share a portion of the load. However, it means learning (and remembering) another complicated knot.

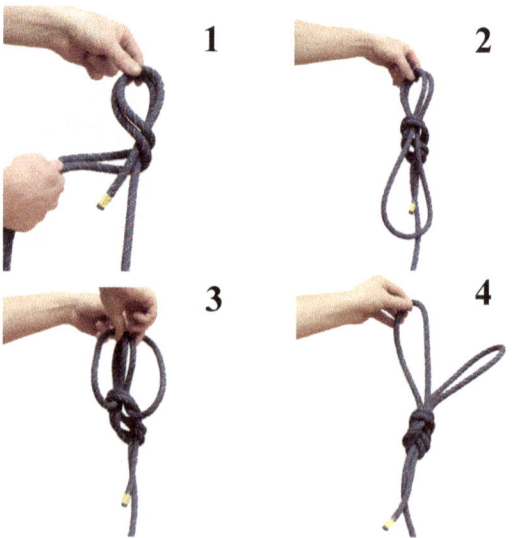

Double-loop figure-of-8 on a bight. Shortening one ear lengthens the other.

TOP ROPE

A fixed rope on a two-bolt anchor

Moving on a fixed rope

To attach oneself to a fixed rope, use either a prusik or an assisted-braking belay device like the Petzl Grigri. When using a prusik, be sure to back it up with either a clove hitch or figure-of-8 on a bight tied in the fixed rope and clipped into your harness belay loop with a locking carabiner.

Prusiking a fixed rope backed up with a clove hitch

To move on a fixed rope, slide the prusik along it with one hand. Let go of the prusik and it will bight into the fixed rope and hold your weight. Always test your prusik to confirm that it bights sufficiently before trusting your life to it. To gain confidence in your system, release the prusik with each step to constantly verify its effectiveness. The advantage of backing up the prusik with a clove hitch instead of a figure-of-8 on a bight is that a clove hitch is adjustable. This allows you to give yourself progressively more slack in the clove hitch without ever undoing it. Prusik along the fixed rope towards cliff edge until you reach the backup clove hitch, hang your weight on the locked prusik as you readjust the clove hitch, snug it tight, then continue to slide the prusik.

If using a Grigri or other assisted-braking belay device on a fixed line, tie a backup knot (overhand on a bight) into the brake strand before you let go of the rope to rig your anchor. This way, if the device unlocks and the rope begins to slip through, it will jam at the knot.

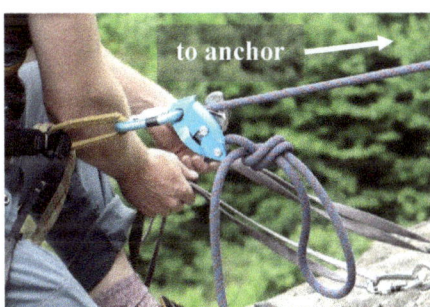

Moving on a fixed rope with a Grigri backed up with an overhand knot

Anchor basics

A belay anchor is a system of slings (or cordelette) and carabiners that attach the climbing rope and thus the weight of the climber to one or several independent anchor points. Belay anchors can be built on natural anchors (trees or boulders), traditional (removable) rock protection, or on permanent bolts drilled into the rock. Here we focus on belay anchors built on either bolts or trees.

43

TOP ROPE

Anchor terminology

- **Individual anchor points:** *bolts or trees*
- **Leg:** *the two strands of sling that run to each anchor point*
- **V-Angle:** *the angle created between the two legs*
- **Shelf:** *A secondary, higher secure point of attachment*
- **Masterpoint:** *the main point of attachment*
- **Dynamic climbing rope**

The main components of a basic belay anchor

Criteria of a good belay anchor

A good belay anchor should respect the following criteria:

1. Strong individual anchor points
2. Equalised
3. Small V-angle
4. Redundant
5. Minimal/no extension
6. Masterpoint extended over the lip
7. Efficient use of gear and time

Strength

The individual anchor points need to be sufficiently strong to withstand the forces generated.

Equalisation

The load should be equally shared between the different anchor points.

V-angle

The anchor must create a "V" between anchor points and not a triangle. The "American Death Triangle" dramatically increases the forces experienced by the anchor points.

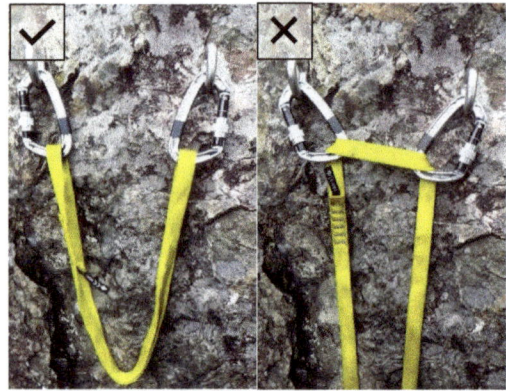

The American death triangle vs V

The V-Angle, (that between the two legs) however must remain small, as the larger the angle, the larger the forces experienced by the individual anchor points. From $0\text{-}20^0$, the two anchor points share the load ~50%-50%, but when the angle is increased to 90^0, each point holds ~70% of the load, and at $150°$, each point is holding nearly 200% of the load! An acceptable V-Angle must be less than $60°$.

TOP ROPE

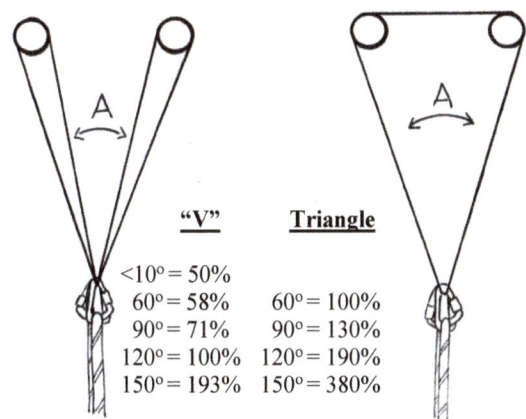

The share of total load held by each leg of an anchor using "V" vs Triangle configurations at different angles

The masterpoint must be extended over the rock lip

Redundancy

If any one component of the system were to fail, (either one strand of webbing, one carabiner, or one anchor point,) there must not be total anchor failure.

Extension and shock loading

Were one of the individual anchor points to fail, the anchor must not extend dramatically and exert a severe shock-load on the remaining anchor point.

Positioning of masterpoint

The anchor must be sufficiently extended such that the rope runs freely and is not in contact with a sharp lip or other feature of the rock.

Efficiency

A good anchor (especially in a multi-pitch scenario) should make efficient use of gear and time.

In reality, it is impossible to perfectly respect all the points listed above, as some of the criteria trade off against each other (ex. a better equalised anchor will have a larger potential extension and vice versa). An anchor should be built for each situation using proper judgement.

A note on slings

Slings pre-sewn in a loop are the strongest, rated to 22kN, and easiest to work with. 18mm nylon is ideal for top rope anchors. Although Dyneema has a greater strength-to-weight ratio than nylon, the tendency for knots in this material to become incredibly tight and difficult to undo after a day of top roping combined with their high cost make them less practical for top rope situations. Furthermore, an overhand knot tied in a dyneema sling can reduce the sling's resistance by up to 50%, whereas nylon retains ~60% residual resistance.

If using un-sewn bulk nylon slings (25mm tubular webbing), you can connect the two ends to make a loop with a water knot (overhand reverse-follow-through). Make sure the knot is dressed and

TOP ROPE

the tails are at least 10cm long (the knot tends to slip over time).

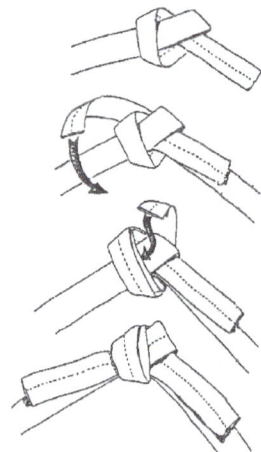

Water knot (overhand reverse follow-through)

Never use a water knot to tie two ends of dyneema together since the slippery material will cause the knot to undo under load.

Anchor-building on bolts

There exist several ways to construct a top rope belay anchor on two bolts, each with its advantages and disadvantages. The following are the simplest and most common.

Two-sling anchor

Two slings of equal length, each attached to one anchor point.

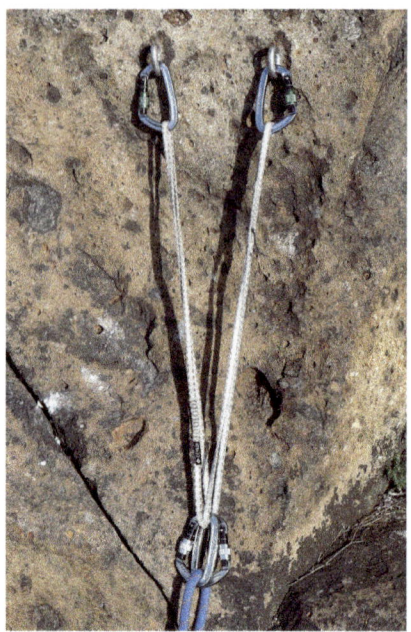

Two sling anchor

*Note that the masterpoint carabiners pass through both slings.

Advantages:
- The strongest (two unknotted slings)
- No extension
- The most efficient use of gear

Disadvantages:
- Only equalised in one direction
- Only possible if the two bolts are at the same height
- No shelf

Strength:
- ~44kN (each leg provides 22kN)

Pre-equalised anchor

The anchor is pre-equalised with a single sling in a V, then an overhand knot is tied to make the sling redundant.

TOP ROPE

Pre-equalised anchor

Advantages:
- Versatile, works on staggered bolts
- No extension
- Has a shelf (clip one strand of each leg)

Disadvantages:
- Equalised in only one direction

Strength:
- ~26kN (one 22kN sling doubled minus 40% due to knot)

To build a pre-equalised anchor, begin by clipping both bolts, pull the sling into a V configuration and then immobilize it in the expected direction of pull. Finish the anchor by tying an overhand knot. (Alternatively, a figure 8 or 9 will also work and will change the final height of the masterpoint.)

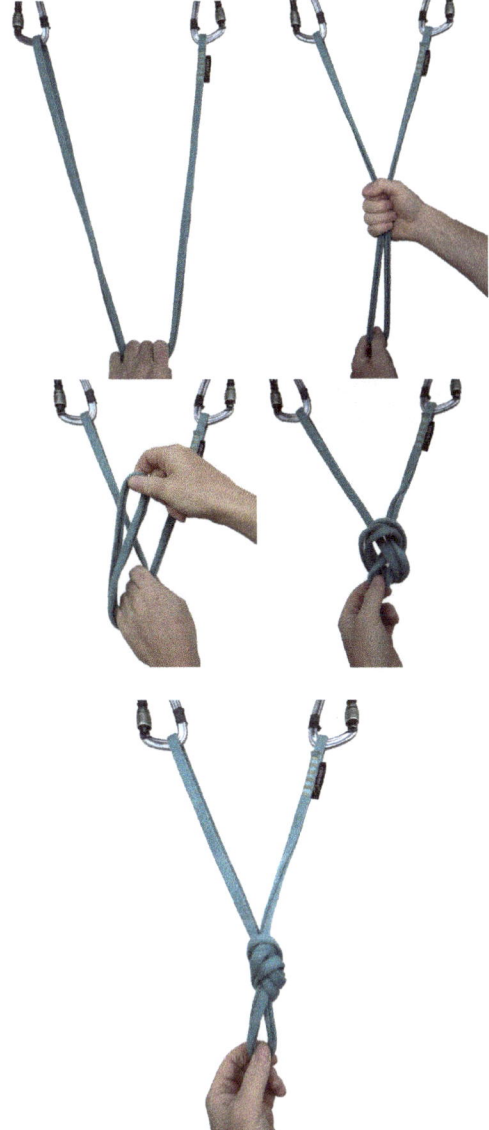
Tying a pre-equalised anchor

Sliding X anchor with extension-limiting knots

A single sling can be used to build a self-equalising anchor, which distributes the load equally between the two anchor points regardless of the direction of pull. Note how the sling has an X twisted into it to make the two anchor points redundant. If one bolt fails, there is not total anchor

TOP ROPE

failure. Extension-limiting knots make the sling redundant and limit potential extension, (while reducing equalizing capabilities).

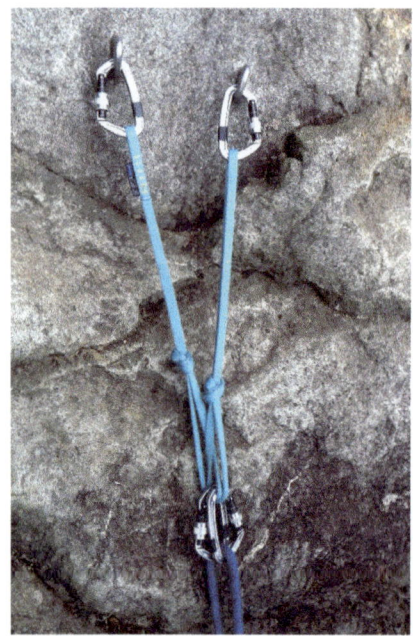

Sliding X anchor with extension-limiting knots

Advantages:
- Self-equalising
- Versatile, works on staggered bolts

Disadvantages:
- Extension if one point fails
- Knots difficult to untie
- Doesn't have a shelf

Strength:
- ~26kN (each leg provides ~13kN, 22kN minus 40% due to knot)

To build a sliding X, begin by clipping one bolt, tie the two overhand knots, then clip the second bolt.

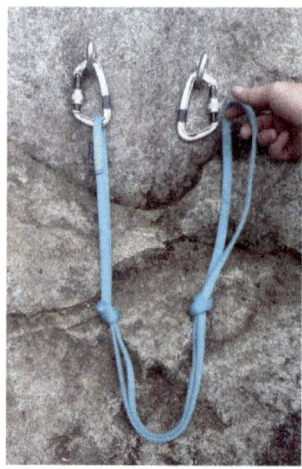

Twist one of the two strands between the knots to create a redundant masterpoint.

Further notes regarding belay anchors

Use of locking carabiners

Locking carabiners attached to bolts should be oriented such that their gates face outwards from each other and screw downwards.

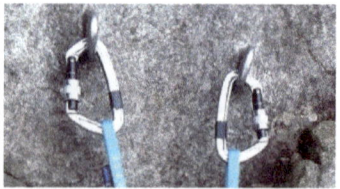

Carabiners correctly positioned on bolts

This ensures that they stay in their strongest axis and that gravity will work to keep the gates shut and not slowly unscrew them. The two locking carabiners holding the climbing rope at the masterpoint should be identical in shape with their gates in opposing directions and screwing downwards.

Gates are opposing and screw downward

Position all carabiners such that they aren't pressed up against a bulge or levered over an edge in the rock. A carabiner placed in this way could snap when loaded.

A carabiner loaded over a rock lip could snap under load

Padding the lip

The masterpoint of the anchor should extend over any rock lip so that the climbing rope runs freely. Furthermore, if the rock lip is sharp, it may also be necessary to pad it to protect the slings from being cut. This can be done simply with an article of clothing or towel that you keep for this purpose. If possible, clip the padding into the anchor rigging so as not to lose it in the wind when the anchor is unweighted.

There are also several rope-protectors on the market that can be used to protect anchor rigging (either sling or rope). Note that you can easily make something similar with an old piece of garden hose slit down the side.

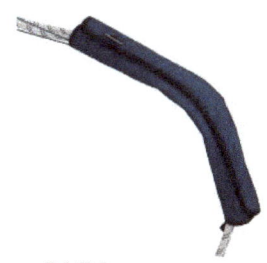

DMM rope protector

Shortening slings

You can easily shorten the length of a sling slightly by wrapping it a couple more times around the carabiner. Although this unknotted sling remains at its full strength, the strength of the carabiner is reduced as it is loaded slightly off its major axis.

A sling is shortened slightly by an extra wrap around the carabiner

Likewise, you can easily adjust the height of the masterpoint by choosing to tie either an overhand, figure-of-8 or figure-of-9 knot. Simply add an extra twist before passing the bight through the loop.

TOP ROPE

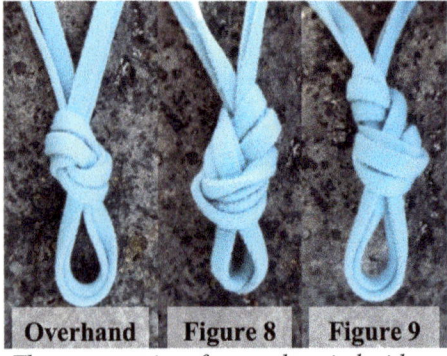

The masterpoint of an anchor tied with an overhand, figure-of-8 and figure-of-9 knot

To shorten a sling significantly, tie an overhand on a bight. Like any knot, this will reduce the strength of the sling. If possible, avoid this by simply doubling the sling instead. The overhand knot is loaded at 180^0.

Overhand knot to shorten a sling

Connecting slings

If a sling is not long enough, it may be necessary to connect two together. The best way to do so is with a locking carabiner.

Residual strength: 100%

Two slings are best connected with a locking carabiner

If a carabiner is not available, it may be possible to tie two slings together directly. However, doing so may decrease their overall strengths dramatically. The residual strength of two connected slings is highly dependent on the specifics (materials, diameters) of the slings used. The following analysis is from a series of QC lab tests done by Black Diamond.

	Girth Hitch	*Strop Bend*	*Comments*
11/16" Nylon & 11/16" Nylon	70%	80%	
12mm Dynex & 12mm Dynex	70%	85%	
12mm Dynex & 11/16" Nylon	55%	55%	Nylon failed
10mm Dynex & 10mm Dynex	53%	58%	Dynex failed
10mm Dynex & 11/16" Nylon	54%	54%	Nylon failed
11/16" Nylon & 10mm Dynex	46%	54%	Nylon failed
8mm Dynex & 8mm Dynex	57%	53%	Dynex failed
8mm Dynex & 11/16" Nylon	56%	57%	Nylon failed
11/16" Nylon & 8mm Dynex	43%	57%	Nylon failed

Residual strength of a variety of slings connected with a girth hitch or strop bend. Data is based on a Black Diamond test that stressed slings statically in a tensile test machine until sling failure, measuring ultimate load. Residual strength (%) is relative to the 22kN CE minimum requirement.

From this data, we can infer that it is safe to attach two slings together directly if and only if they are of the same material and same large diameter. Tying two slings together of different diameters will greatly decrease their strengths as the smaller diameter sling will cut into the larger. Skinnier 8 and 10mm Dyneema slings should be avoided, and since 12mm Dyneema is rare in comparison, it is best to conclude that ***only two nylon slings of the same diameter should ever be tied together.***

TOP ROPE

The preferred knot to attach two slings together with is the symmetrical strop bend.

Residual strength: ~80%

Strop bend

Although very similar to a girth hitch, the strop bend retains a slightly greater residual strength of the sling (~80% compared to ~70%). Whereas the asymmetrical girth hitch involves one sling hitched around the other, the strop bend is symmetrical with each sling holding the other, increasing its strength. Symmetrical and without crosses, the stop bend is essentially a well-dressed girth hitch.

The residual strength of an 8mm Dyneema sling tied to a 18mm nylon sling with a girth hitch is only ~50%.

Residual strength: ~50%

A Dyneema sling girth-hitched to a nylon runner is dangerous

Since the safety of tying two slings together depends on several nuances, in general it is safer to avoid altogether. Simply carry enough carabiners to use as intermediate links.

Anchor-building on trees

Trees, (or boulders) can be extremely strong and make great natural anchor points.

Choosing trees

For a tree to be used as an anchor point (in a two-point belay anchor), it must respect the following criteria:

- >15cm in diameter at base
- Alive
- Solid (give it a good push)
- Well-rooted (roots not exposed from erosion)

Make sure to sling the tree at its base to reduce leverage.

If a tree meets all the above criteria and is > 40cm in diameter at its base, it is sufficient to be used as the sole anchor point for a belay anchor.

One-tree anchors

The best choice, if the sling is long enough, is to wrap it around the tree then tie a knot (overhand, figure 8 or figure 9) to make the sling redundant.

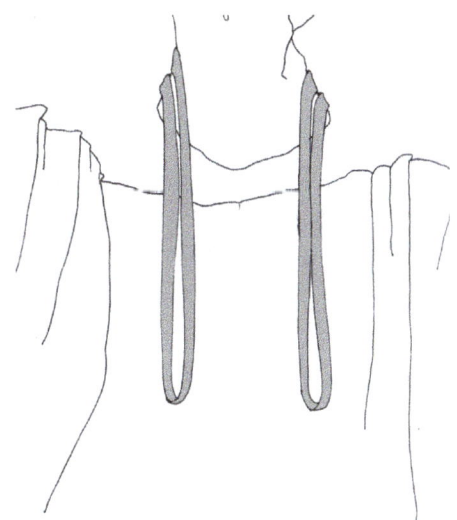

TOP ROPE

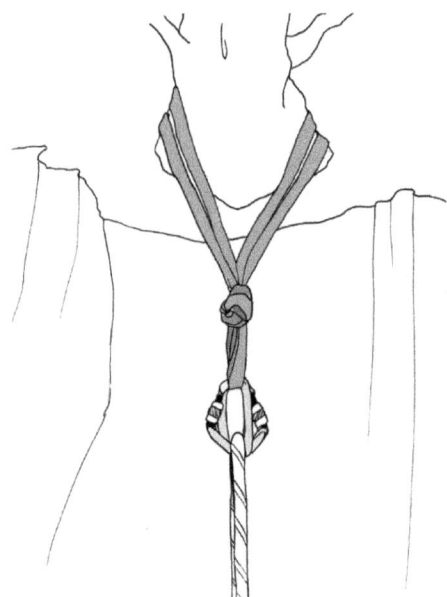

One sling made redundant with a knot

Another possibility is to simply girth hitch the tree. This anchor can be made redundant by using two separate slings. The advantage is that there are no knots to untie at the end of the day.

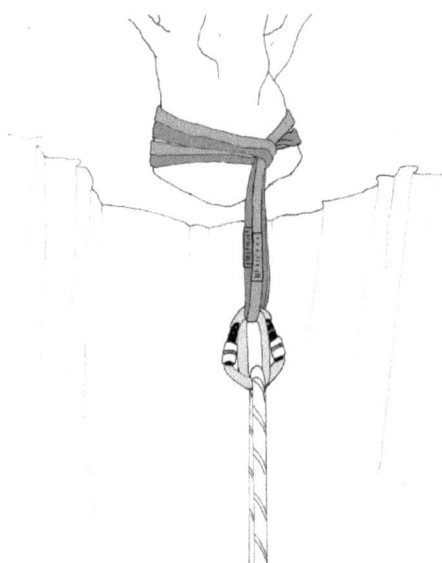

Girth hitch with two slings

Two-tree anchors

Remember that the two trees must be close enough to each other as to create an acceptable V angle (less than 60^0). Start by slinging each tree with a girth hitch, clip each sling with a locking carabiner, then proceed with the same logic as though each tree were a bolt.

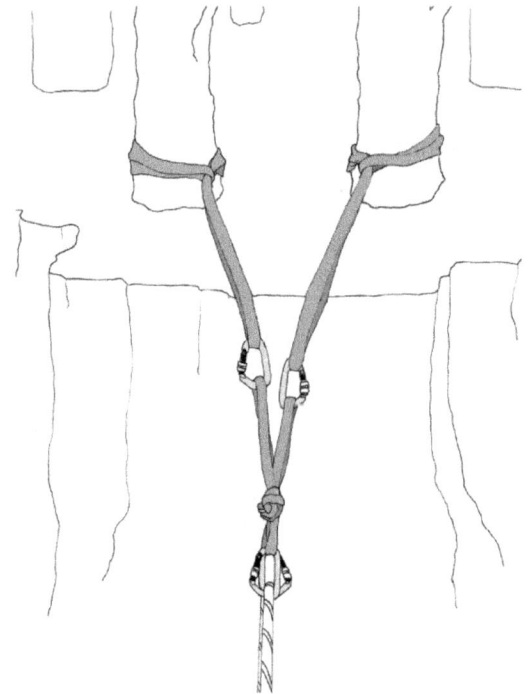

A pre-equalised anchor on two trees

For this to be feasible, the trees must be close to cliff edge, and you may need a large length of webbing.

Extended anchors

If the nearest suitable tree(s) are set well back from cliff edge, it will be necessary to build a well-extended anchor. Although this can be done with several pre-sewn slings connected, it is often easier to use either bulk unsewn 25mm tubular nylon webbing or a length of static climbing rope.

TOP ROPE

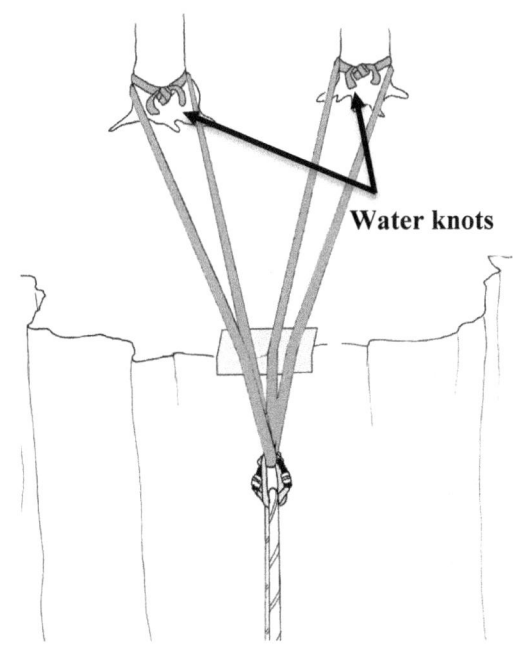

Belay anchor built using unsewn tubular webbing. As always, be aware of the slings running over sharp rock. Here the lip is padded to protect the webbing.

Since a water knot decreases the strength of the sling, it is best (but not essential) to double wrap the tree and position the water knot against the tree where it will experience the least force. This will also make the knot easier to untie afterwards.

<u>Anchor building using static rope</u>

The most versatile method of building belay anchors on trees is by using a long (20-30m) piece of static rope. It is important that the rope is static and not dynamic since a dynamic rope running over sharp rock will stretch back and forth each time it is weighted, increasing the chances of it cutting as the same section of rope under tension saws back and forth over the rock. Never hesitate to pad the lip if the rock is sharp.

To construct a belay anchor on two trees with static rope, first fix the rope to the first tree with a rethreaded figure-of-8, measure the right distance and tie two figure 8s on a bight to create a redundant masterpoint, then clip the other leg into a sling girth-hitched to the second tree using a clove hitch. Using a clove hitch makes it simple to adjust the length of the leg when equalising the anchor. Be sure that the tail of the rope is sufficiently long (>1m) and the clove hitch snugged tight.

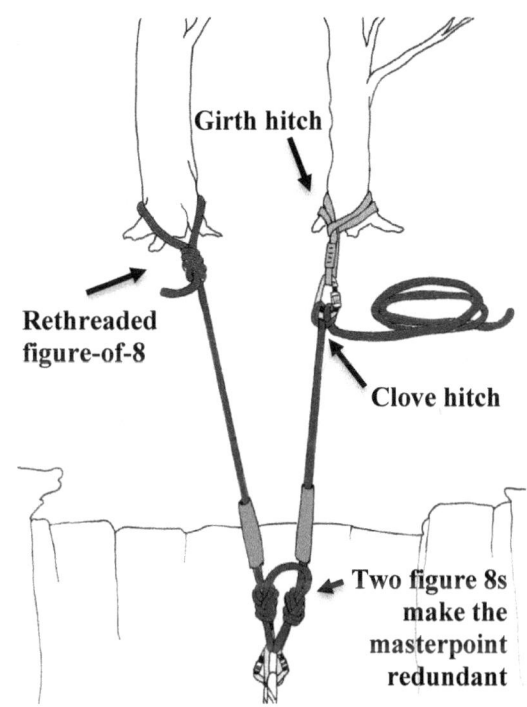

Belay anchor on two trees built using static rope. Note that two rope protectors enclose the static rope at the lip.

TOP ROPE

A redundant masterpoint made with two separate figure 8 knots

Belay anchor on one tree built using static rope

This configuration is practical since you can use the rope as a fixed line to keep yourself safe while you're building the anchor. After securing the first leg of the anchor, you can prusik your way to cliff edge to measure out the masterpoint.

The same method can be used to build an extended anchor on a single tree set far back from cliff edge. After setting the masterpoint (two figure 8 knots), bring the second leg of the anchor back to the same anchor point.

If there are only marginal trees available, (~15-20 cm in diameter,) you may choose to build a three-tree anchor. Start by fixing the static rope to the first tree with a figure 8 follow-through. Girth hitch the two other trees with slings. Pass the rope through the locking carabiner of the second tree then clove hitch it to that of the third.

TOP ROPE

Ground anchors

If the climber weighs significantly more than the belayer (~50%), the team may choose to anchor the belayer to the ground. Ground anchors are also useful in situations where the belay terrain is dangerous (such as on a small ledge), or if for whatever reason, the belayer would like to be positioned further away from the route than would be normally acceptable (for example to avoid standing in a puddle, in the hot sun, next to a wasp nest, etc.). Remember that the ground anchor must be strong in the expected direction of pull, and the belayer must be positioned along this axis to prevent a jolt in the event of a climber fall.

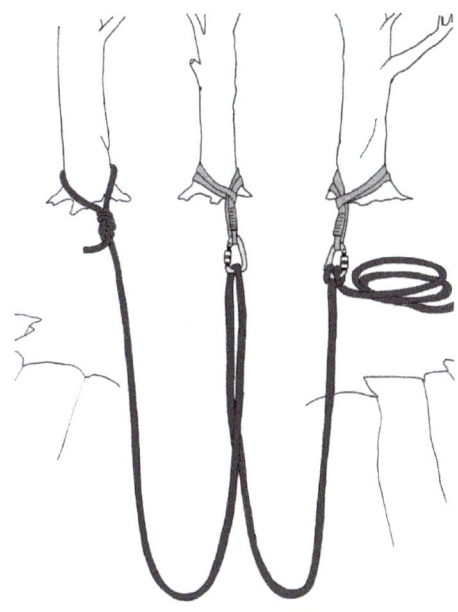

To create the masterpoint, tie one big figure 8 knot in both loops.

The simplest ground anchor consists of slinging a tree with a girth hitch and using the climbing rope to attach yourself to it with a clove hitch on a locking carabiner.

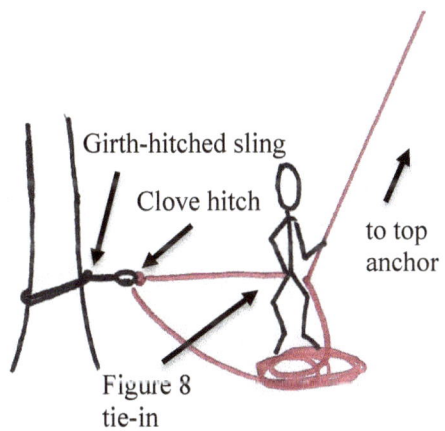

Belayer tied into a ground anchor

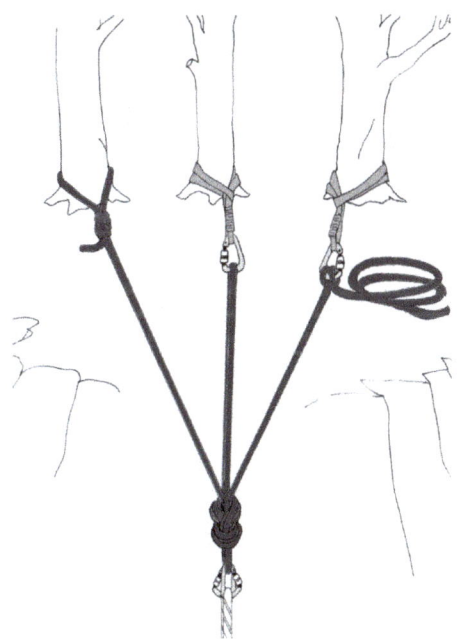

Belay anchor on three trees built using static rope

Since this anchor is not critical, (failure will not result in catastrophe,) and will experience smaller forces, the seven anchor criteria discussed earlier may be interpreted more loosely (sling redundancy is not necessary for example).

TOP ROPE

The rule of redundancy

Now that the concept of redundancy has been discussed in relation to belay anchors, it is important to elaborate. The failure of any one piece of equipment must never result in catastrophe. This is achieved by always backing everything up such that the entire system is never dependent on a single element. This rule of redundancy applies for all equipment in all situations with the exceptions of:

- The climbing rope
- The harness belay loop
- The belay device
- The dynamic personal tether
- A locking carabiner that is within arm's reach (ex. for belay device or personal tether)
- A really big tree (that meets the criteria discussed earlier in this chapter)

Thus, when switching systems, for example from a fixed-rope system to clipping in directly to an anchor, to setting up a rappel, be sure that you are always clipped into a redundant system.

Rappelling

After the top rope anchor is built, you have two options to get down, hiking or rappelling. If the hike is long and tedious, then rappelling will be the preferred option. Likewise, to get back to the ground after climbing the route, rappelling can be a better choice than lowering if the rope runs over sharp edges or overly textured rock that could damage the rope.

Lowering and rappelling differ in two fundamental ways. Firstly, lowering requires a belayer whereas for rappelling, the climber descends autonomously. Secondly, lowering involves the rope fixed to the climber's harness and sliding through the anchor system (and over the rock), whereas for rappelling it is the climber that slides down the unmoving rope which runs through the anchor as a double strand. Therefore, if the rock is sharp, lowering can be dangerous, (although care must also be taken when rappelling).

Although rappelling generates only relatively low forces (no falls, only body weight), it is a high-risk activity because you are continuously testing your safety system and have no room for error. Studies reviewing accident reports consistently show that rappel accidents are responsible for a high proportion of all climbing-related deaths.

The recommended rappel set-up is with the rappel device extended by clipping it to the short tail of the personal tether and backed up with a prusik clipped to the belay loop. Note that the prusik is tied around both brake strands simultaneously. Extending the rappel device on a personal tether (instead of being clipped directly to the belay loop as was traditionally done,) reduces the risk of having hair, clothing or gear jam in the device while descending, and allows the prusik to act more reliably by blocking fully before coming into contact with the rappel device.

Rappelling with the device extended on the short tail of the personal tether backed up with a prusik

Most rappelling-related accidents can be categorized as either rappel-anchor failure, losing control of the rappel, or rappelling off the ends of the rope. Because any rappel error will likely result in catastrophe, it is essential to use good practices to reduce these risks. First, to reduce the chance of losing control, always use a prusik back up. This way, if for whatever reason, you let go of the brake strands, the prusik will prevent you from falling. Second, always tie stopper knots in the ends of both strands before rappelling. Even if you're certain that the cliff is shorter than 30m (half a rope's length), if the rappel rope is not centered in the anchor, you could rappel off one end of the rope, sending you plummeting. Finally, be certain that the anchors are sufficiently strong.

Key points for rappelling

- Always back up your rappel with a prusik (or other friction hitch).
- Make sure the prusik is short enough that it blocks before it reaches your rappel device.
- Always tie stopper knots in the ends of your ropes.
- Always double-check your rappel set-up before unclipping yourself from the anchor.
- Always rappel (instead of lower) if your rope is running over sharp edges.
- As you descend, place your rope to avoid sharp edges and sideways slips that could damage the rope and/or cause rockfall.
- Never pass your rope directly through bolt hangers, (only glue-in bolts, quicklinks or rappel rings).
- Always double check the state of the fixed rappel anchors. Rap rings can become worn very quickly if parties practise the bad habit of top roping or lowering directly through them.

Before unclipping your tether and trusting your life to your rappel set-up, test your rappel by taking up all slack, sliding your prusik up and transferring your weight to the rappel. Your prusik should bite the brake end of the ropes before it reaches the rappel device. If so, you can let go of the brake end to give yourself confidence that your set-up works. After unclipping your tether from the anchor, always keep a hand on the brake end of the ropes, even with a prusik. If you need to let go for whatever reason, you can tie a knot (overhand on a bight) into the brake strands as a backup or wrap the ropes three times around your leg (old-school method). Photo examples of rappelling can be found at the end of this chapter.

Rappelling off an anchor that is beneath you

If building a belay anchor from above, lower your weight onto it carefully (personal tether clipped to masterpoint) to avoid a fall onto the static anchor. As intermediate attachment points, the anchor has 1. individual anchor points 2. the shelf 3. the masterpoint, and your harness has 1. the belay loop 2. the short leg of the personal tether 3. the long leg of the personal tether. Gradually lower your weight in small intermediate steps so that you are always under tension on your anchor.

Alternatively, you may decide to remain on your fixed line as you descend to the anchor, or even rappel off a higher anchor (a monolithic tree) to reach the belay anchor in question, retrieve your rope, then set up a second rappel to get down. Untie the stopper knot before pulling the rope and tie the rope to yourself so you don't drop it.

Climbing and belaying

Once the rope is set up, the subsequent techniques, tying in and belaying, are similar to those practised indoors but with some subtle yet important differences.

Tying in

The preferred knot for the climber to tie into the rope with is the figure 8 follow-through (rethreaded figure-of-8). Start by tying a figure 8 knot, pass the rope through the two harness tie-in points (not the belay loop), then rethread the 8.

Figure 8 follow-through tie-in

Since the figure 8 is doubled, there should always be two parallel strands running next to each other through the entire knot- two running in, two running out, and three pairs of two parallel strands visible on each side. The FQME (Québec Climbing Federation) proposes 6 additional criteria to verify a well-tied figure 8 knot:

1. The rope passes through the correct two harness tie-in points
2. The distance between the harness and the knot is not more than 10cm
3. The knot is properly dressed (without strands crossing)
4. The knot is snugged down
5. The tail of the rope exits the knot through the V created by the knot's outer loop
6. The tail of the rope is at least 10cm but not longer than 20cm

Many climbing cultures accept or even teach sloppy undressed tie-in knots with crossing strands and an excessively long tail. Although it is not essential for the figure 8 follow-through to be dressed in order to be safe, when well-dressed, it is easier to inspect and slightly stronger than one with crossed strands. Similarly, keeping the tail in the V of the knot protects the standing end of the rope when the knot tightens. Tying a compact knot that is close to your harness and without a long flapping tail makes everything more enjoyable, reducing the chances of being whipped in the face or of clipping the wrong part of the rope into protection when lead climbing. The minimum tail length of a well-tied, snugged-down figure 8 knot is 10x the diameter of the rope, about 10cm for a standard rope. A tie-in knot whose tail is too short is potentially dangerous due to the risk of it untying.

To ensure that the tail is long enough but at the same time to keep it out of the way, a second backup knot may be tied after the first figure 8. The best choice is a stopper knot (half of a double fisherman's) tied tight against the figure 8. Even better is to master tying the figure 8 follow-through with the perfect 10-20cm tail, no stopper knot required.

TOP ROPE

A half-double fisherman's (stopper knot) backing up a figure 8 tie-in knot

Rigging the belay device

For a traditional tube or plate belay device such as the ATC, the rope is installed by taking a bight of rope and inserting it through either of the device's two slots. The brake end of the rope should pass through the teeth of the device (designed to increase friction) and point outwards from the belayer. The belay locking carabiner (ideally pear-shaped) should be clipped to the ATC cable, the rope and the harness belay loop without creating any twists in the belay loop.

A correctly rigged ATC

Always clip the belay device to the belay loop and not to any other point on the harness, (such as the tie-in points which would load the carabiner tri-axially).

Belay basics

Belaying means the unconditional agreement that you are at all times prepared to catch a climber fall, expected or unexpected. Using a tube or plate device (like an ATC), the three fundamentals of belaying are to:

1. Always remain in complete control of the brake end of the rope,
2. Remain in the open position (low friction) for the shortest possible time before blocking with the brake hand below the belay device, and
3. Manage the rope to keep the appropriate amount of slack in the system.

Now let me elaborate on each point.

Being in complete control of the brake end of the rope means always having at least one hand holding it (and only it) with a closed fist and thumb wrapped around the rope. Under no circumstance should this first priority be sacrificed. The hand holding the brake strand is called the "brake hand" and should be the belayer's dominant hand. The other hand is called the "guide hand."

Regardless of whether the rope is under tension, the blocked position refers to holding the brake end of the rope lower than the belay device (or technically, where the device will position itself once under tension, about 10cm above the belay loop).

59

TOP ROPE

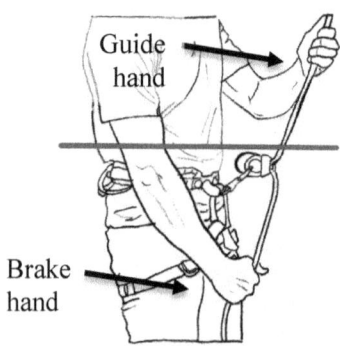

The blocked position means holding the brake strand lower than the height of the bely device when under tension, here denoted with a red line

Holding the brake strand in the blocked position will easily generate enough friction to hold a fall, whereas holding the brake strand above this point will eliminate nearly all friction and make catching and holding a fall next to impossible. When taking in slack, it is necessary to temporarily pass through the open position before returning to the blocked position. Be sure to do this only briefly, never hesitating with the brake hand above the belay device.

If ever slack builds up because the climber ascends faster than the belayer can take it in, it is important to communicate with the climber for them to stop climbing while the belayer takes in the excess slack. Whereas a little too much slack indoors means only a slightly longer, but likely still safe fall, outdoors, this could result in the climber hitting a ledge or bulge.

Belay sequence

The neutral position should be with the brake hand on the brake strand in a blocked position and the guide hand high on the rope, ready to take in slack. (Keep ~5cm between the device and your brake hand to avoid having your skin pinched.) Once there is slack in the rope,

A. Raise your brake hand to the open position and pull the slack through the device, pulling both up with the brake hand and down with the guide hand at the same time.

B. Immediately return to the blocked position with the brake hand lower than the belay device

C. Temporarily grab the brake strand with the guide hand (either above or below the brake hand)

D. Slide (or walk) the brake hand back up to return to the neutral position.

The variations in steps C and D (expressed in parentheses) represent regional differences in belay technique. They are all adequate, so long as the three fundamentals of belaying are always respected. It's best that you stick to only one technique to develop solid belay reflexes.

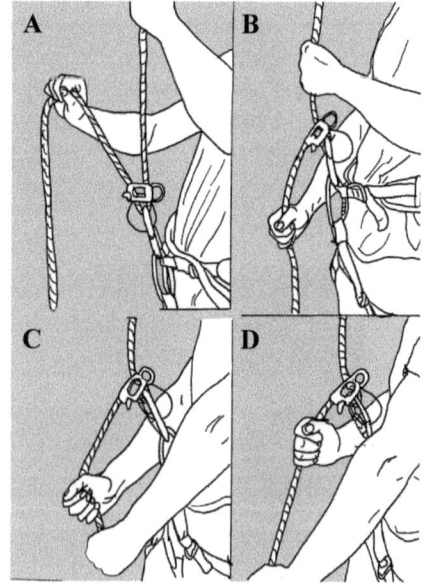

The basic belay sequence

Belayer positioning

In addition to respecting these three basic rules, the belayer must also position themselves correctly. This means ideally standing within 2m of the base of the route (or more precisely, from the point on the ground directly under the top anchor).

If the belayer is positioned too far to the side or back from the cliff, a climber fall could pull the belayer up, sending them flying dangerously towards the rock. This is especially true if the climber is heavier than the belayer.

Many climbing gyms have top rope anchors where the rope wraps 1.5x around a cylindrical beam (aka belay bar). This "double wrap" drastically increases friction and therefore reduces the force felt by the belayer. Although this increases safety, it is also a false sense of security that can result in bad belay habits. Since an outdoor top rope anchor consists of the rope running through only two carabiners, the friction is far less. Therefore, impeccable belay technique is a must and proper positioning essential.

Weight differences

Since the belayer acts as a counterbalance to hold the climber, the belayer must have a minimum weight relative to the climber. Because of the friction created by the rope running through the top anchor, a lighter belayer can get away with belaying someone up to ~1.3x their weight without being pulled into the air (for an explanation of the pulley effect, see forces and physics in Chapter 4). More than this however and caution should be exercised. The belayer must be prepared to be pulled upwards in the event of a fall. Once the climber weighs ~50% more than the belayer, the belayer may no longer be able to hold the climber's fall without being pulled violently upwards. The team should then consider building an anchor for the belayer to hold an upward pull. If belaying while anchored, be sure that you are positioned directly between the anchor and the expected direction of pull so that a climber fall won't pull you in an unexpected or dangerous way.

Rope stretch

Because an outdoor climb is usually significantly longer than an indoor one, the increased amount of rope in the system results in far greater potential rope stretch. At the beginning of a 30m top rope climb there is 60m of rope in the system. A standard rope with ~8% static elongation means falling up to nearly 5m when your belayer takes you tight. This is also exaggerated by the reduced amount of anchor friction outdoors compared to indoors (no double wrap) and is potentially dangerous given the presence of boulders or uneven, rocky terrain at the base of routes. The belayer should keep the rope extra tight for the first few meters of the climb, or whenever the climber is above a bulge or ledge.

Partner check

Before the climber leaves the ground, it is essential to practise a partner check. The belayer should verify that the climber's harness is correctly worn, that the figure 8 knot is well-tied and that the ropes don't twist over themselves at the anchor. The climber should verify that the belayer's harness is correctly worn, the belay device installed correctly, and the belay carabiner locked. Finally, check that neither climber nor belayer are wearing dangerous jewelry. Climbing while wearing a ring could mean losing a finger, belaying with loose long hair could mean having to cut it after it gets sucked into the belay device, and climbing with a long necklace is clearly a bad idea. Remove such jewelry and tie long hair back.

Catching a fall

So long as you're respecting the 3 fundamental rules of belaying, (in complete control of the brake end of the rope in a blocked position and without excess slack,) and are positioned correctly, a fall should be easy to hold. Like belaying indoors, a belayer's reflex should be to pull downwards on the brake end of the rope firmly. A good general rule is that at any point when the climber is weighting the rope, (immediately after a fall, if the climber asks to be taken tight, or during the descent,) the belayer should hold onto the brake strand with both hands for added security. Also, since the outdoor belay terrain is often uneven and

TOP ROPE

unstable, it is good practice for the belayer to wear closed toe shoes to ensure a solid stance.

Belaying with an assisted-braking device

The Petzl Grigri or other such assisted-braking devices can be a good choice for top rope belaying outdoors. In the event that the belayer loses control of the brake end of the rope due to a falling rock, wasp sting, a slip on a wet rock, etc., an assisted-braking device could mean the difference between dropping the climber or not. If you do choose to belay with an assisted-braking device, be sure to belay with proper technique and not allow laziness and complacency to take over. Many accidents are caused from people belaying poorly with assisted-braking (formerly called auto-locking) devices.

When using an assisted-braking device, ensure that the rope is compatible with the device. Small diameter ropes won't engage the cam and thus won't block as surely as with thicker ropes. Thread the rope correctly in the device and follow all other recommendations of the manufacturer of the specific device.

Top rope belay technique should be identical to that with an ATC, except the descent is controlled with a mechanical lever. This is when accidents often happen. The lever disengages the cam completely, the rope slips through the device with little friction, burning the belayer's brake hand who then drops the rope and down comes the climber. To avoid this, control the speed of descent by opening the lever only partially, with the brake hand on the rope only as a backup. If the climber is descending too quickly, let go of the lever, not the rope.

Communication

The basic communication used at the beginning of an indoor climb consists of:

"Am I on belay?"
   "The belay is on."
"May I climb?"
   "Climb on."

Often shortened to just: "Climbing" - "Climb on." Further commands are:

- "Take" (take the rope tight as I'm about to let go)
- "Up-rope" (Take some slack out of the rope but not total tension)
- "Slack" (Give me some slack)
- "Lower" (Let me down)

with logical corresponding responses. Keep communication concise to avoid misunderstandings. If there are other climbing parties nearby, it is best to precede any command with your partner's name to avoid all confusion, e.g., "Bartholomeus! Slack!"

All of this is identical outdoors with the addition of a few important commands. If and when a rock or pebble is knocked loose and begins to fall, yell "rock!" Even if it's not a rock (maybe a piece of gear or a stick or anything else), the accepted convention remains to yell "rock". If you're on the ground and hear this yelled, you may want to look up to see if you can dodge the incoming projectile, or you may prefer to stay put to avoid a rock in the face. On steep terrain, stepping towards the cliff is the best option. Hopefully you're wearing a helmet.

The climber calls "secure" when they are clipped in directly to the top anchor and want the belayer to take them off belay completely (if they intend to rappel). It's not a bad idea for the belayer to confirm this with the climber before acting. After the belayer detaches their belay device, calling "off belay" confirms to the climber that they are no longer being belayed and that the rope has been freed from the belay device.

Before tossing the rope down from the top of the cliff, call "rope!" to inform those below.

TOP ROPE

Cleaning the belay anchor

The last person to climb a route must retrieve the anchor gear, either to build a belay anchor elsewhere or to pack up the gear for the day. If you rappelled earlier then your fixed line is likely still in place. In this case, simply put yourself back on the fixed line, clean the belay anchor, then use the fixed line to regain safe terrain before cleaning the fixed line and hiking down. However, the opposite is also possible, to have first cleaned the fixed line and hiked down before climbing the route. In this situation you are obliged to clean the belay anchor and descend on rappel.

Cleaning and rappelling – sequence

Whereas there are many possible sequences to execute this transition, they are all governed by a few underlying principles and priorities:

- The transition should be kept as simple as possible to avoid error
- The transition should use the minimum necessary equipment to reduce clutter
- Each step should be logical, a series of small, ordered objectives leading to the big picture objective
- Communication with the belayer should be clear and minimal to avoid confusion
- The plan should be discussed by both partners before leaving the ground
- The rule of redundancy should always be maintained throughout the transition

Order of objectives

1. Clip yourself in directly to a redundant system then call "secure"
2. Clip the rope to yourself so as not to drop it
3. Untie your knot, pass the rope through the rappel anchors
4. Set up your rappel (with stopper knots and a backup prusik)
5. Double check the system then clean the anchor
6. Descend on rappel

Step by step

1. Clip yourself in directly to one of the two bolts with your personal tether

2. Unclip one of the two anchor carabiners

3. Clip to belay loop. You're now independently attached to each bolt

TOP ROPE

4. "Secure!"

5. Clean up the anchor so that there is only one carabiner in each bolt

6. Pull up a bight of slack and tie a knot

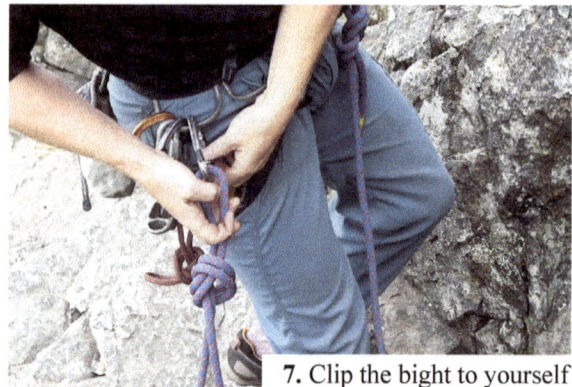

7. Clip the bight to yourself

8. Untie your figure 8 knot

9. Thread the anchors

TOP ROPE

10. Tie a stopper knot

11. Untie the rope from yourself

12. Center the middle of the rope

13. Tie a second stopper knot

14. Set up your rappel (with prusik backup)

15. Double check everything, then clean the anchor

16. Before unclipping your tether, weight your rappel to insure your prusik bights

17. Descend on rappel

If you need to let go of the rope and aren't convinced by your prusik's efficiency, you may choose to tie an overhand on a bight as a backup.

TOP ROPE

Overhand on a bight used to back up a rappel

Essential equipment checklist

All climbing equipment must be certified by either the UIAA or CE.

- Dynamic single-rated climbing rope, suggested length 60m, diameter 9.8-10.3mm
- ~30m static rope (diameter 9-11mm) for fixed-rope anchor system and anchor rigging on trees
- Pre-sewn 18mm nylon slings for anchor (suggested: 1 x 240cm, 2 x 120cm)
- 6 shared locking carabiners (4 for basic anchor plus 2 extra for complex anchor or fixed line)
- 3 personal locking carabiners (for belay device, personal tether and prusik)
- Dynamic personal tether (either pre-made, or DIY with ~2.5m of climbing rope)
- Prusik loop (made from 1.5m of 7mm cordelette)
- Something to pad the lip with (old t-shirt, towel, or rope protectors)
- Climbing helmet
- Tube-style belay/rappel device
- Assisted-braking belay device (optional)
- Harness
- Shoes
- Chalk bag
- A friend

*Out beyond ideas of wrongdoing and rightdoing,
there is a field. I'll meet you there.
When the soul lies down in that grass,
the world is too full to talk about.
Ideas, language, even the phrase "each other"
doesn't make any sense.
The breeze at dawn has secrets to tell you.
Don't go back to sleep.
You must ask for what you really want.
Don't go back to sleep.
People are going back and forth across the doorsill
where the two worlds touch.
The door is round and open.
Don't go back to sleep.*

-Rumi

Chapter 4 – Single-pitch sport climbing

Lead climbing differs from top roping in that instead of the rope running through a top anchor, the leader secures it into intermediate protection points while climbing. Sport climbing, one style of lead climbing, refers to climbing routes protected entirely by permanent bolts instead of the traditional practice of placing removable protection on the lead. Because clipping solid bolts is easier and safer than having to worry about how to protect a route while simultaneously figuring out the moves, sport climbing has enabled the sport to progress quickly to an impressively gymnastic level.

Sport climbing grew out of the mid-1980s when French climbers, impressed by the high standard of climbing developing at Yosemite, California, were inspired to put up routes of comparable difficulty in France. However, since French limestone was much harder to protect naturally with chocks than Californian granite, these climbers began liberally bolting routes, until they were entirely protected by bolts alone. When these bolting practices made their way back to the United States, they were first met with much resistance by traditionalists who waged a war over climbing ethics. One side saw bolts as a way to make climbing more accessible, fun and safe, while the other saw them as a sacrilegious and short-sighted assault on the rock, permanently scarring it and at the same time taking the adventure out of climbing. Bolts were placed, bolts were chopped, but eventually, both sport climbing and traditional climbing have come to coexist (mostly) peacefully. Moreover, sport climbing has opened up numerous new and previously "unclimbable" crags, helping disperse growing crowds caused by the recent surge in popularity of the sport.

In Québec and North America more generally, the general ethic is that if the route is protectable traditionally, then it should remain natural, but if not, then it's bolted. Therefore, on rock types that produce an abundance of crack systems, (notably granite,) bolts are rare, but on limestone and other sedimentary rock types, sport climbing dominates. Finally, mixed routes exist where a route is partially protected traditionally, but bolts protect the run-out blank sections. Note that ethics may vary locally between regions.

Although at first glance, sport climbing appears very similar to lead climbing in the gym, there are several significant additional hazards outside as well as other essential techniques that are beyond the scope of indoor lead climbing.

Differences between leading inside and outside

The most marked difference between leading indoors and outdoor sport climbing is the distance between the bolts. Indoors, permanent quickdraws are placed at short intervals that make falls always short and safe, (provided you have a competent belayer). This is not necessarily the case outdoors as bolts are sometimes widely spaced. Routes are generally bolted by the first ascensionist party and it is their discretion where and how many bolts to place. Local climbing ethics come into play, and often routes will be under-bolted in sections where the climbing is easier, (although this older ethic is changing). Sometimes bolts are placed at awkward and inconvenient spots because that is where the rock quality was best. Sometimes a route is simply poorly bolted. Sometimes, even if the route is well-bolted, ledges and pendulums make falls potentially dangerous. Sometimes the most dangerous part of a climb is simply getting to the first bolt, 5m up with a rocky landing beneath you! The fundamental change that needs to happen when transitioning from the gym to outdoor sport climbing is a psychological one. A leader must be constantly assessing risk and evaluating the

SINGLE-PITCH SPORT CLIMBING

consequence of a potential fall at any point. Never take safety for granted.

A sport climbing crag is not a climbing gym and it is your responsibility to evaluate every bolt you clip into. Most bolts on popular sport routes are in good condition, but it is possible for bolts to fail, and very possible for old bolts to fail. Old school bolts from the 1980s or before, button heads (the end of the bolt looks like a convex coat button), those with a star stamped on the end, or any sort of funky homemade bolt hanger, should not be trusted. Never have complete faith in a bolt if it is rusted, if it moves in the bolt hole or if it is set in bad rock, close to a crack system or arête. When in doubt, find a safe way to escape and choose a route with better hardware. (Review the section on bolts in Chapter 1 for more on bolt assessment and quality.) Likewise, never have complete faith in a permeant draw hanging from a bolt without inspecting it first. Nylon draws wear quickly from exposure to the elements and metal draws can rust or become worn from use. As always, thoroughly inspect everything you trust your life to.

Before leaving the ground

- Make sure your rope is long enough for the route. Almost all pitches are bolted with a 60m rope in mind (max 30m), although some long pitches require a 70m rope.
- **Always tie a stopper knot into the other end of the rope.** In case the rope is too short, this will prevent the belayer from dropping the climber while lowering. (Alternatively, as practised in multi-pitch climbing, the belayer can tie into the other end of the rope.)
- Count the number of bolts from the ground and bring enough quickdraws plus an extra in case you drop one.
- Communicate with your belayer and make a plan for when the climber reaches the top. Be sure to have the gear necessary for anchor manipulations.
- Obviously, don't forget the partner check, confirming the climber's figure 8 knot is tied correctly, both harnesses are worn correctly, and the belay device is correctly installed with the belay carabiner locked.
- If the first bolt is unreasonably high, it can be clipped from the ground using a stick clip ("cheater stick") to avoid a ground fall. Stickclips can be purchased, or you can make your own out of a long stick, a twig, and some tape.

An improvised stickclip

Lightly tape the upper carabiner of the quickdraw to the end of a stick, prop the gate open using a small twig and clip the rope to the lower carabiner making sure not to back clip. Clip the quickdraw to the first bolt, pull the stick away and you're ready to climb the beginning of the route on top rope.

SINGLE-PITCH SPORT CLIMBING

Clipping the first bolt with an improvised stick clip

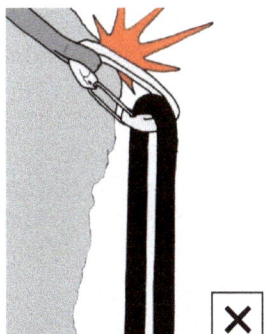

The quickdraw here is too short

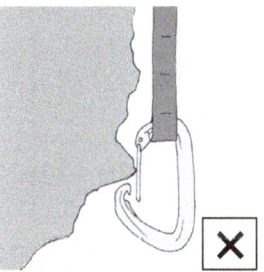

The quickdraw here is too short

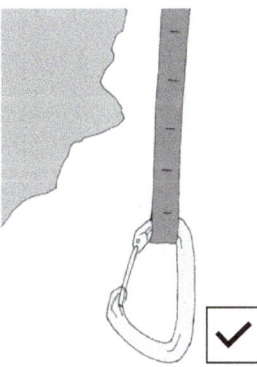

A long draw extends the carabiner over the bulge

Clipping

Clipping bolts can be broken into three steps:
1. Choosing the quickdraw,
2. Clipping the quickdraw to the bolt, and
3. Clipping the rope to the draw.

Choosing the quickdraw

The carabiners of the quickdraw must lie flat against the rock (or hang in air) and not be inhibited by protruding rock features. If the carabiner is lying on a bulge in the rock, a leader fall could open the gate or load it on a dangerous axis, potentially causing the carabiner to break. Instead, clip the bolt with a longer quickdraw. Always carry one or two longer quickdraws for such situations.

Quickdraw orientation

- The (often curved gate) carabiner fixed tightly to the sling is intended for the rope, the loose carabiner is to be clipped to the bolt. Clipping a quickdraw upside down increases the chances of rope drag pulling

69

the upper carabiner into a cross-loaded position on the bolt. To prevent this, when racking, always clip the bolt end of the quickdraw to your harness gear loops.
- Pay attention to not mix your carabiners up. A carabiner slightly damaged by repeated contact with bolts can easily damage a rope if used at the rope-end of a quickdraw.
- If the route climbs straight up, the quickdraw can be oriented with the carabiner gates facing either right or left. If however the next stage of the route traverses slightly to the right or left of the bolt being clipped, it is best to clip the quickdraw with the gate direction (of both carabiners) opposite from the progression of the leader. This decreases the chances of both the upper carabiner cross loading in the bolt, and the rope unclipping from the lower carabiner in the event of a fall.

Gate direction should be opposite from the progression of the leader

A quickdraw incorrectly oriented can cause the upper carabiner to cross load in the bolt or flip upwards, increasing the chances of the carabiner either snapping under load or unclipping from the bolt

Clipping the rope

The rope should always progress from the rock, out through the quickdraw carabiner, to the climber. The opposite is known as a "backclip."

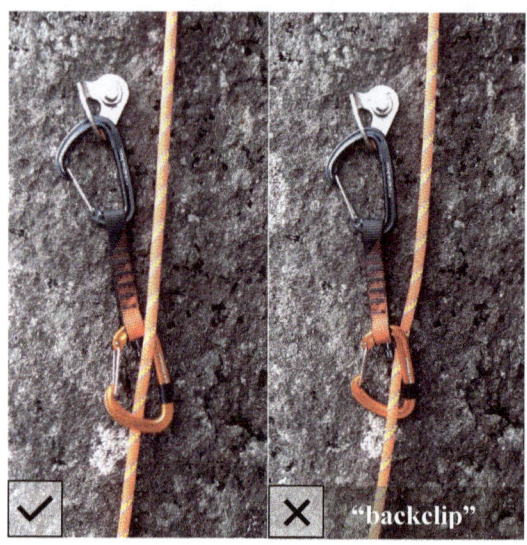

Backclipping a quickdraw is dangerous as it could result in the rope unclipping itself from the draw during a leader fall.

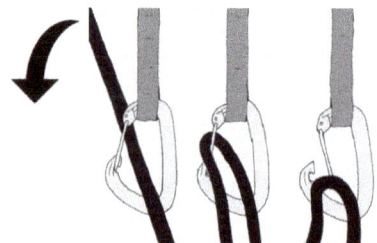

Backclipping a quickdraw greatly increases its chances of unclipping

Footwork

When lead climbing, it is imperative to keep the rope in a position such that it won't trip the climber in the event of a fall. If the rope runs behind the climber's leg, it could flip them upside-down, burning their leg and potentially sending them swinging headfirst into the rock.

Here the rope runs dangerously behind the climber's leg

Lead belaying

Lead belaying is founded on the same basic concepts as top rope belaying with a few important differences. Using a tube device (like an ATC), the three fundamentals relevant to both top rope and lead belaying are to 1. Always be in complete control of the brake end of the rope, 2. Remain in the open position (low friction) for the shortest possible time before blocking with the brake hand below the belay device, and 3. Manage the rope to keep the appropriate amount of slack in the system.

Like for top rope, at least one hand must always be holding the brake strand with a closed fist and thumb wrapped around it. When holding the brake strand in the blocked position, the belay device will easily generate enough friction to hold a fall, but in the open position, with the brake hand above the belay device, the absence of friction makes even holding the climber's weight next to impossible (see the section on top rope belaying for elaboration). When taking in slack (as in top rope belaying), it is necessary to temporarily pass through the open position before returning to the blocked position. However, when giving slack, one should always remain with the brake hand lower than the belay device, ready to catch a fall. The correct amount of slack to keep in the rope is the minimum possible without ever having the leader feel tension. This is especially true early on in the route where too much slack could mean the leader hitting the ground. Leave a small bend of slack in front of you to grant the leader unrestrained movement.

Top rope vs. lead belaying

Besides the obvious difference of direction (taking in slack for top rope vs. paying it out for lead) belaying a leader involves several unique considerations. Lead falls can easily generate 2-4 times the force of top rope falls which are rarely more than a couple of kN (body weight + pulley effect + very short falls). Remaining in control of the brake end of the rope is thus considerably harder and special care should be taken to always have a firm grip, no matter what.

Specific to lead belaying

The three priorities while lead belaying in order of importance are to:

1. prevent the leader from hitting the ground or a ledge,
2. protect yourself as the belayer, and
3. provide the softest catch possible, (lower the force of impact).

In addition to the three fundamentals of belaying listed earlier, the belayer should also stay within 1m of the beginning of the route and position themselves to prevent getting pulled into the rock and the leader falling further than necessary.

SINGLE-PITCH SPORT CLIMBING

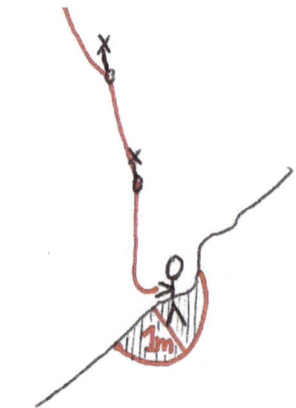

Avoid belaying outside a 1m radius from the start of the route (first quickdraw)

To prevent a leader-belayer collision, for the first 6m or so of the route, the belayer should never stand directly underneath the climber, but instead slightly to one side or the other (while still within the 1m radius).

As the leader progresses, the potential danger can be assessed at both the macro and micro levels. At the macro level, the danger is greatest when the climber is low on the route. This is because a fall could result in hitting the ground or the belayer, as well as the fact that the shorter amount of rope in the system will act more statically and result in a more violent catch. As the climber gains height, the chance of hitting the ground diminishes and a fall of the same length will be softer due to the longer amount of dynamic rope in the system. At the micro level, the greatest risk is when the leader is above their previous bolt and pulling out slack to clip the next one. If the leader falls before clipping the rope, the fall will be long. As a belayer, when giving slack for the leader to clip, we can do three things to mitigate this risk:

- Approach the wall as much as possible, eliminating any extra rope in the system,
- Remain in a position ready to reel in the slack if ever the leader doesn't succeed in clipping the draw
- Remain completely attentive until the quickdraw is clipped.

If the leader drops the slack without having clipped, the belayer can quickly reel in a few armslengths of rope before returning to the blocked position. In the worst-case scenario where the leader peels off with the unclipped slack still in their hand, the belayer can quickly reel in one armslength of rope and dash backwards and down to shorten the length of the fall. Although a rare situation, a belayer must always be ready for this possibility.

Forces and physics

A force, measured in Newtons (N), is an interaction that causes a mass to change its velocity (accelerate or decelerate). A falling climber accelerates due to the force of gravity acting perpetually downwards, and then the climber decelerates due to the opposing force of the climbing gear resisting the force of gravity. Once at rest, the force of gravity is perfectly balanced with all opposite forces holding/pulling the climber upwards.

In a top rope scenario simplified as a static environment (without falls) the force of the climber weighting the rope is determined by Newton's second law:

$$F = ma$$

where the force is equal to the climber's mass multiplied by the acceleration of gravity (constant = 9.8m/s/s). Therefore, a climber of 60kg exerts a force of ~600N or 0.6kN. Because the belayer's weight is also felt by the top anchor, in a frictionless world, the belayer would exert a subsequent 0.6kN on the top anchor. Because of the friction of the rope running through the carabiner, the actual contribution of the belayer due to such a pulley effect is only a fraction of the climber's, around 2/3, so the actual force experienced by the top anchor is roughly 1.66× the weight of the climber. In this case, 0.6kN contributed by the climber (F_c), and 0.4 kN contributed by the belayer (F_b) result on a total of 1kN on the top anchor.

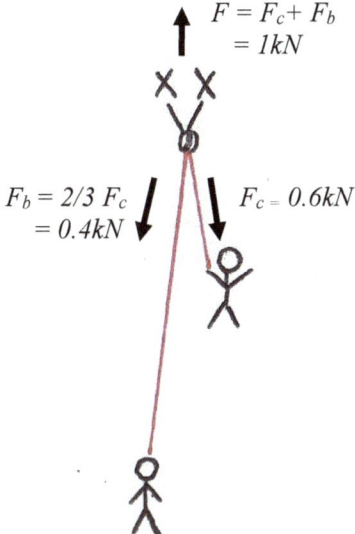

The pulley effect

In a lead climbing scenario where the leader takes a long fall, forces can be considerably higher, similar to jumping on the bathroom scale and watching your weight double.

The climber begins falling at point A, accelerates to a maximum velocity at point B where the rope begins to catch the fall and then decelerates to point C where the climber is at rest.

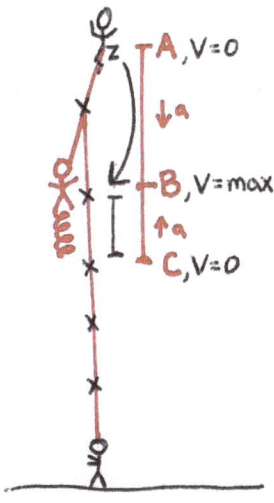

Physics of a leader fall

If we were to calculate the forces involved in this fall using F=ma, the acceleration in question would not be the gravitational constant, but the magnitude of the deceleration from points B to C. This deceleration is really a ratio of two factors: the initial maximum speed (equivalent to the length of the fall) and the length of the period of deceleration (how dynamically or statically the fall is caught) described by:

$$a = \frac{V_{max}}{t}$$

where V_{max} is the velocity at point B and t is the time between points B and C. So the force required to slow a moving mass (the climber) is:

$$F = m \left(\frac{V_{max}}{t}\right)$$

and in a vertical world where the force of gravity is always acting downwards, the force felt by the top anchor during a lead fall is:

SINGLE-PITCH SPORT CLIMBING

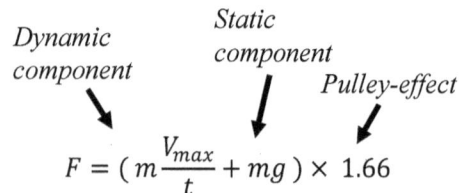

$$F = (m\frac{V_{max}}{t} + mg) \times 1.66$$

Simplified to:

$$F = 1.66m(\frac{V_{max}}{t} + 9.8)$$

Although this explanation assumes that the deceleration is constant throughout the catch, which is not necessarily true, it is helpful in exposing all important variables involved, namely: the mass of the climber (m), the length of the fall (V_{max}) and the length of the period of deceleration (t). Besides the climber's mass, it is really just the ratio between A-B and B-C. If this ratio doesn't change, then the force remains the same. As a belayer, to decrease the force of a given fall, since we can't change the mass of the climber, we can then either shorten A-B or lengthen B-C. A-B, the length of the fall is determined by the height of the climber above the last bolt, but also by the amount of slack the belayer has in the rope. B-C, the length of the catch is determined by the elasticity of the rope, the amount of rope in the system (the more rope involved, the more potential stretch), the catch itself (including the belay device used, the difference in weight between the climber and the belayer, and the belay technique employed). So, for a given leader fall, we can keep less slack in the system beforehand to shorten the length of the fall, and we can catch more dynamically to soften the impact.

The fall factor

The most important element in the system to dynamically absorb the energy of a leader fall is the climbing rope. For a given fall of 2m (from 1m above the last bolt), what will most determine the amount of force generated is the height of the climber on the route. When the climber is high on the route with more rope in the system, the elastic potential of the rope is large and will easily elongate to slow the falling climber. However, for the same fall low on the route, the rope has less elastic potential and acts more like a static rope, greatly increasing the forces felt by the climber, belayer, and top-anchor point.

Therefore, the severity of a fall can be estimated using a value called the fall factor, calculated as the length of the fall divided by the length of rope in the system, and will be roughly proportional to the amount of force generated.

$$Fall\ Factor = \frac{length\ of\ the\ fall}{length\ of\ rope} \propto F$$

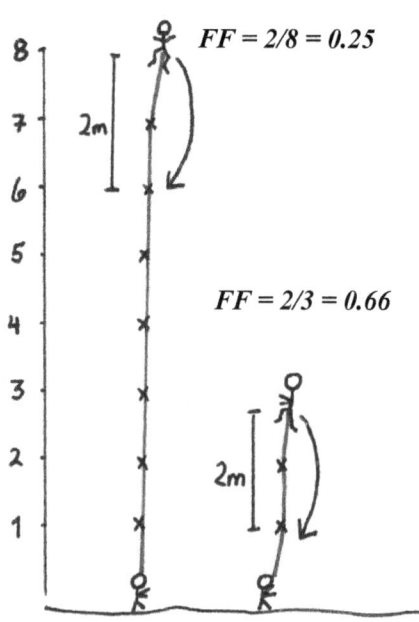

Two identical falls of 2m with different corresponding fall factors. The second fall has a fall factor of more than twice the first and will consequently likely generate more than twice the force.

Dynamic vs. static belaying

Besides the dynamic properties of the rope, the belay method can greatly increase or decrease the amount of force generated by a leader fall. The belayer can decide to catch the fall either statically or dynamically. A static catch shortens the length of the fall but increase the forces, whereas a dynamic catch lengthens the fall but gently brings the falling leader to a halt.

The two methods to catch dynamically are to 1. let a certain amount of rope slip through the belay device during the fall, and 2. to lightly jump upwards during a fall to act as a travelling counterweight to the falling leader. Both techniques should be mastered and can be used independently or in combination.

Going back to the three basic priorities of the belayer, one should always catch as dynamically as possible provided that it doesn't result in 1. the leader decking (hitting the ground or a ledge,) or 2. the belayer getting hurt (colliding with the leader or being pulled up into a bulge or roof). Climbing with the same partner regularly will help your ability to judge intuitively how dynamically you can belay in different situations.

Weight differences

A good rule of thumb is that the climber shouldn't outweigh the belayer by more than 30%. When the belayer is heavier than the climber, the catch will be more static so the belayer must pay attention to catch more dynamically to compensate. However, when the belayer is significantly lighter than the climber, the catch is always dynamic as the belayer will be yanked up violently towards the first bolt. In situations where it is important to catch more statically (such as low on the route), having a light belayer could mean the climber hitting the ground. 30% is relevant because it is roughly the amount of friction added to the system by a rope bending over the single carabiner of the highest quickdraw. If the climber weighs more than this and there is no other friction in the system, the belayer may never fully stop the falling leader (before being sucked into the first bolt). If the leader weighs more than 30% more than the belayer, the belayer can anchor themselves to the ground (although this will dramatically increase forces,) or a friction-increasing quickdraw such as the "Ohm" by Edelrid can be used to clip the first bolt.

The "Ohm" by Edelrid

Note that the Ohm should not be used in traditional climbing since it relies on an unquestionably strong and multi-directional first piece of protection to be effective, which isn't always available without bolts. Beware of using a camming assisted-braking device when belaying a significantly heavier leader. If the belayer gets pulled all the way into the first quickdraw, the carabiner could press against the cam causing it to disengage and the device to unlock.

Belaying with the Petzl Grigri

Although here is not the place to go over the nuances of belaying specific to each of the many belay devices on the market, given the popularity of the Petzl Grigri in the sport climbing community as well as its often-incorrect usage, it is worth writing a few words about it. Assisted-braking belay devices are great tools to reduce objective risks like rockfall and can facilitate the belayer's job when the climber is working a route. If rockfall were to cause the belayer to lose control of the brake strand,

SINGLE-PITCH SPORT CLIMBING

the device's braking mechanism could prevent a ground fall, and when a leader repeatedly hangs on the rope, such a device assists the belayer in holding the climber's weight with only minimal effort. Given that hangdogging is a common style to work sport routes, and that bolts are more than strong enough to withstand the increased fall impact force caused by the sudden braking action, assisted-braking devices are a good choice for sport climbing.

The danger comes from the fact that with all assisted-braking devices, in order to give slack quickly (for example when the climber needs rope to clip), it is necessary to temporarily deactivate the device's braking mechanism. If the climber falls at this moment, then there is a chance that the device will fail to lock resulting in a dangerous fall. For the Petzl Grigri, recommended belaying techniques have changed over the years prompted by the occurrence of many such accidents. When giving slack for the climber to clip, it is imperative that the belayer remains in control of the brake strand. Keep 3 fingers around the rope, while the index finger supports the device, and the thumb depresses the cam. Note that the index finger should only ever support the device under the lip and never under the device itself. If the Grigri is pinched between the thumb and index finger, or even worse, gripped by the entire hand, the cam will not engage during a fall.

The only correct position to hold the Petzl Grigri when needing to disengage the cam to quickly give slack

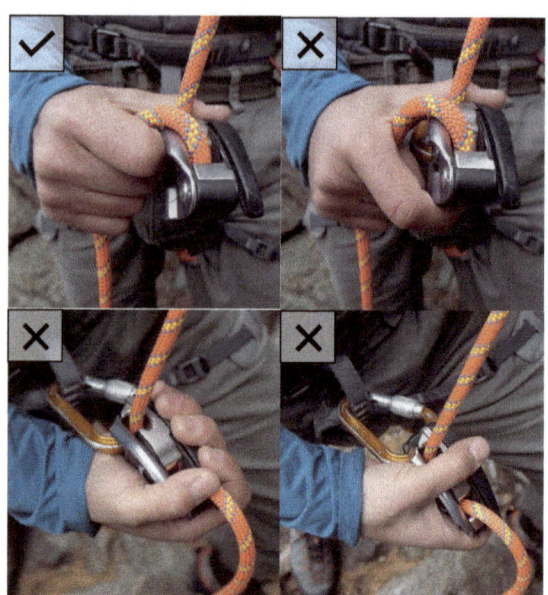

Holding the Grigri incorrectly could result in a ground fall

To master the nuances of lead belaying technique with any device, it's best to seek qualified instruction. In addition to reading the manufacturer's information booklet, when first belaying with a new device, ask a staff member at your local climbing gym to confirm your belay technique.

What to do once at the top

The first thing to do once you get to the top of a route is to make yourself safe by clipping into the anchor. This can either mean clipping your rope into a draw in one of the bolts and having your belayer take you tight, or it can mean clipping into a bolt directly with your personal tether.

On clipping into the anchor directly

To make yourself truly secure, you need to be clipped into a redundant system. Never trust your life to a single bolt. If you clip into only one bolt, make sure to also stay on belay. More generally, always respect the rule of redundancy (explained in the previous chapter).

Just because you are secure (clipped in directly to a redundant anchor), doesn't mean you should necessarily call "secure" to your belayer. This is a serious mistake that has resulted in several fatalities. Remember "secure" is a command asking your belayer to completely detach their belay device. Only call this if you're going to descend on rappel.

When clipped in directly to the anchor, always keep your weight on your tether to prevent the possibility of shock loading the anchor.

Once at the top you have three options, depending on whether your partner is also wanting to climb the route: 1. lower off quickdraws at the anchor leaving all gear in place for your partner to lead, 2. build a belay anchor for your partner to top rope off of, or 3. pass your rope directly through the anchor and descend without leaving gear behind.

Lowering

If your partner is to lead the route next and doesn't mind preplaced draws, simply clip one or both anchor bolts with quickdraws, call "take", and lower like in the gym.

Building a belay anchor

If your partner is to climb the route next on top rope, build a belay anchor on the two bolts. In addition to the different belay anchors described in the previous chapter, it is common on sport routes to build a belay anchor with two quickdraws. It's best to use at least one quickdraw with locking carabiners.

Two-quickdraw anchor

A belay anchor made from two quickdraws, one of which has locking carabiners. Gates are oriented outwards.

Advantages: Very fast and efficient

Disadvantages: Only works if the two bolts are at the same height and close together (to prevent a large V-angle).

After building a belay anchor, you then have the option to:

A. Belay from above (as for multi-pitch climbing, explained in Chapter 5), or to
B. Belay from the ground (in which case you must either rappel or have your belayer lower you).

Passing the anchor

If you are the last person to climb the route, you will want to descend without leaving gear behind. Assuming there are acceptable fixed anchors to pass the rope through, you will need to clip in directly to the anchor, untie your knot, pass the rope through the fixed anchors, then set up to either be lowered or to rappel.

SINGLE-PITCH SPORT CLIMBING

Lowering technique 1 – Sequence

1. Clip into both bolts with your personal tether

2. Ask your belayer for slack, ("slack!") then pull up a couple meters of rope

Note: Your partner keeps you on belay. **Do not call "secure"**.

**Here the position can be made more comfortable by extending the short tail of the personal tether with a spare quickdraw. Note that since the entire system is not dependent on just the quickdraw, it is acceptable for it to use non-locking carabiners.

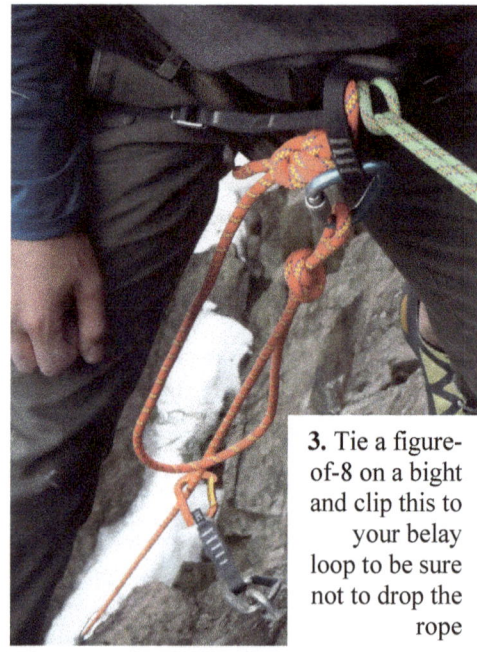

3. Tie a figure-of-8 on a bight and clip this to your belay loop to be sure not to drop the rope

Note: if you use a locking carabiner, this provides an extra backup, given that you're still on belay.

SINGLE-PITCH SPORT CLIMBING

4. Untie your initial tie-in knot

5. Pass the rope through the anchors

6. Rethread your harness tie-in knot

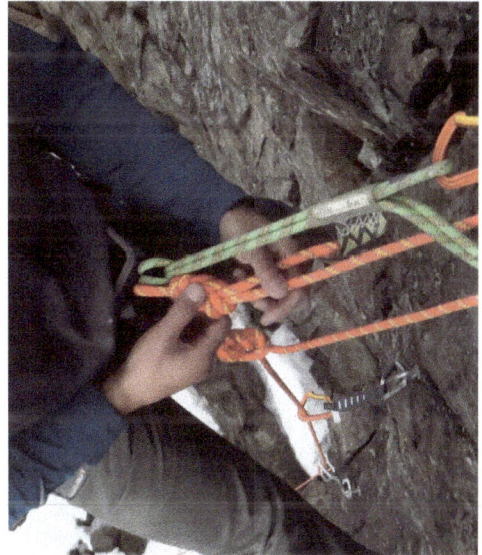

SINGLE-PITCH SPORT CLIMBING

7. Untie the figure-of-8 clipped to your belay loop

8. Call "take!" and weight the rope

9. Double check your knot, then unclip yourself and lower

Lowering technique 2 – Sequence

For this alternative technique, after clipping into the anchor, instead of untying first and then passing the rope through the anchors, here, (after clipping into the anchor) you first pull up slack, pass a *bight* of rope through the anchor points, and then clip a figure-of-8 on a bight to your belay loop with a locking carabiner. Since you're still being belayed on your initial harness tie-in knot as you thread the anchors, this method is arguably safer. Although it's always best to start by clipping in directly to both bolts, the presence of a reliable backup could justify clipping into only a single anchor point. If you are unsure of whether you need to clip into one or two bolts, consider the rule of redundancy and ensure you are never entrusting your life to a single element in the system.

1. Clip into one or both bolts with your personal tether

SINGLE-PITCH SPORT CLIMBING

2. Ask your belayer for slack, pull up a bight of rope and thread it through the anchor points

4. Untie your initial tie-in knot and pull the strand out from the bolts

3. Tie a figure-of-8 on a bight and clip it to your belay loop with a locking carabiner

SINGLE-PITCH SPORT CLIMBING

5. Call "take!" and weight the rope

6. Double check your knot, then unclip yourself and lower

*Note – this technique only works if the anchor hardware is large enough to permit you to pass a bight of rope through which is not the case for chains or small quicklinks.

Rappelling

Similar to "lowering technique 1", but instead of asking for slack, your belayer will take you completely off belay (the command is "secure") so you can pull half the rope through the anchors and rappel. Refer to the sequence described in the previous chapter in the section "Cleaning the belay anchor".

Notes on passing the anchor

Several variations of these sequences exist. Regardless of the specifics,

- Discuss your plan with your partner before leaving the ground,
- Make sure you have enough gear for the sequence,
- Keep communication clear,
- Never call "secure" if you want to be lowered
- Never trust your life to a single bolt,
- Always keep your rope attached to something to avoid dropping it, and
- Always double check your set-up before untying your knot, calling "secure", or unclipping your personal tether from the anchor.

To rappel or to lower

Whether you should rappel or lower depends on the steepness of the pitch, your plan to recover quickdraws, if the rope runs over sharp rock features, and on the type of fixed gear at the belay station. If the rope runs over sharp edges, you should rappel, as lowering could severely damage or cut your rope. Rappel carefully placing your rope where it is protected, away from sharp rock. Lowering will always put more wear on anchor hardware due to friction created by the rope running through the anchor under tension. It is therefore often more considerate and respectful to descend by rappelling. When the climbing community spends

SINGLE-PITCH SPORT CLIMBING

time and money bolting and equipping routes with fixed gear, the hope is that it will last for a long time. Consider the type of anchor hardware the rope is running through:

- ***Personal gear*** – lowering is faster than rappelling and makes it easier for you to retrieve the rest of your quickdraws, especially on traversing or overhanging routes.
- ***Quicklinks*** – Inexpensive and easily replaceable, without changing the bolts. Therefore, lowering off these is acceptable. If you see severely worn quicklinks at the anchor, replace them with new ones (UIAA/CE certified).
- ***Rap rings*** – Only lower off rappel rings if they are attached to the bolts with quicklinks (and can therefore be easily replaced). Often rap rings can't be replaced without changing the bolt hangers as well.
- ***Glue-in bolts*** – lowering off glue-in bolts is a crime as wear on the bolts will necessitate the anchor to be re-bolted as a result. If you want to lower, leave two quicklinks behind.

Never pass your rope directly through bolt hangers which could cut the rope.

Whatever your decision, make sure to clearly communicate your intentions to your belayer, ideally before you leave the ground.

Cleaning draws

After leading a route, you can either clean the quickdraws on your way down (lower or rappel), or you can leave them in place for your partner to clean as they climb on top rope. If the route is generally a straight line, the quickdraws are easy to clean and can be done so by any of the 3 methods mentioned above. However, if the route is traversing, is overhanging, or has a roof, cleaning the draws can be tricky to do on rappel and should therefore be done by lowering or by the second.

The second cleans

If your partner is planning to top rope the climb, the easiest is to have them clean the draws on the way up. First build a proper belay anchor and have your partner lower you. Your partner then ties into the strand that runs through the draws and unclips and cleans them as they ascend. This works especially well on overhanging or traversing routes since in order to top rope it, the draws would need to stay in to act as "directionals" anyway to prevent a pendulum swing.

Cleaning while being lowered

In order to stay close enough to reach all of the quickdraws, clip one end of a quickdraw to your belay loop and the other to the belayer's end of the rope. This is called tramming.

Tramming

**Be careful when you unclip the final (lowest) quickdraw. This could send you and your belayer

SINGLE-PITCH SPORT CLIMBING

on a dangerous pendulum swing. It is often best to simply lower to the ground, then re-climb the beginning of the route with a spotter to retrieve the first draw.

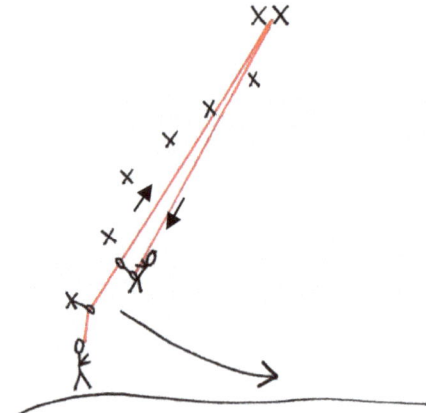

When tramming a traversing or overhanging route, cleaning the first draw could result in a dangerous pendulum swing

Cleaning on rappel

Although cleaning on rappel is much harder than cleaning while being lowered, your partner on the ground can help you retrieve quickdraws out of reach by pulling the strands of your rope when you need. As always, back up your rappel with a prusik.

Bailing off a bolt

If you're not able to finish the route, you'll need to bail off your high point. This requires you to leave some gear behind to lower off of. Instead of leaving expensive quickdraws, you can carry a quicklink or two on your harness for this purpose.

1. Have your partner take you tight on your last bolt

2. Clip yourself directly into the bolt, all the while staying on belay

SINGLE-PITCH SPORT CLIMBING

3. Transfer your weight onto your tether by asking for slack, then clean the quickdraw

4. Replace the quickdraw with a quicklink

5. Have your partner take you tight

6. Unclip your personal tether

** You should avoid trusting your life to a single bolt. One option is to leave a second quicklink on the second highest bolt. Alternatively, you can attach a prusik to the belayer's side of the rope, clipped to your belay loop with a locking carabiner, and slide it down as you're lowered. In the event that the upper bolt blows, the prusik will catch your fall on the next closest bolt.

SINGLE-PITCH SPORT CLIMBING

7. Install your prusik and lower

- Personal locking carabiners x 3 (for belay device, personal tether and prusik)
- Climbing helmet
- Tube-style belay/rappel device
- Assisted-braking belay device (optional)
- Harness
- Shoes
- Chalk bag
- A friend

> *You are not a drop in the ocean*
> *You are the entire ocean in a drop*
>
> -**Rumi**

Essential equipment checklist

All climbing equipment must be certified by either the UIAA or CE.

- Dynamic single-rated climbing rope, suggested length 60m, diameter 9.6-10mm
- 8-12 short quickdraws
- 1-2 long quickdraws
- 2 draws with locking carabiners (optional)
- Anchor gear (120cm or 240cm sewn nylon sling & 4 locking carabiners)
- Stickclip (optional)
- Two quicklinks (UIAA/CE certified)
- Dynamic personal tether
- Prusik loop (made from 1.5m of 7mm cord)

Chapter 5 – Multi-pitch sport climbing

This chapter goes hand in hand with Chapter 6 – Self-rescue, a mastery of which is essential to becoming autonomous in multi-pitch climbing

Multi-pitch climbing can provide a tremendous amount of satisfaction. The exposure, feeling small and stranded out on a sea of rock, is for many the quintessential climbing experience. But with this exposure comes significantly more risk. In single-pitch situations shorter than 30m (using a 60m rope), you can always lower the leader to the ground if the route is too hard, or in the event of an accident. In multi-pitch climbing, getting off a route, especially with an injured partner, can be incredibly complex. A party climbing a multi-pitch route must therefore be completely self-sufficient and competent in self-rescue techniques and basic first aid in addition to the basic techniques of multi-pitch climbing, belaying, and rappelling.

Preparation

Making a plan

Before leaving the ground, the party must discuss their plan of ascent and descent.

- Will one leader lead all the pitches, or will the two partners swing leads?
- Are all pitches shorter than 30m? If not, does the leader trail a second rope (tag line)?
- Might communication be a problem? Do you have rope-tug signals worked out?
- What is the best way to descend (rappel or walk off)?
- If planning on rappelling, does the rappel line require two ropes?
- Are there sections of the route from which it is easier or more difficult to bail?

What to bring

Besides the technical equipment necessary to get up and down the route, a team may need to bring a number of additional supplies up a wall with them including:

- Water
- Food
- A headlamp (even if you expect to be down by lunch time)
- Extra layers (a waterproof shell in case of a change in weather)
- Shoes if the plan is to walk off
- A small first aid kit
- Sun protection
- Rescue gear
- Cell phone (and relevant phone numbers)

Both climbers may thus need to climb with backpacks, or perhaps, one backpack between the two, worn by whoever is seconding.

Multi-pitch belay anchors

Belay anchors on multi-pitch sport routes will nearly always be built on two bolts, (or possibly a good tree after topping out onto a ledge).

Pre-equalised

A pre-equalised anchor provides two secure and redundant points to clip into: the masterpoint and the shelf. To clip the shelf, clip one strand of each leg of the anchor. In a multi-pitch situation, this is useful to reduce clutter as at one point there will be both climbers, the belay device, and maybe a backpack all clipped into the anchor.

MULTI-PITCH SPORT CLIMBING

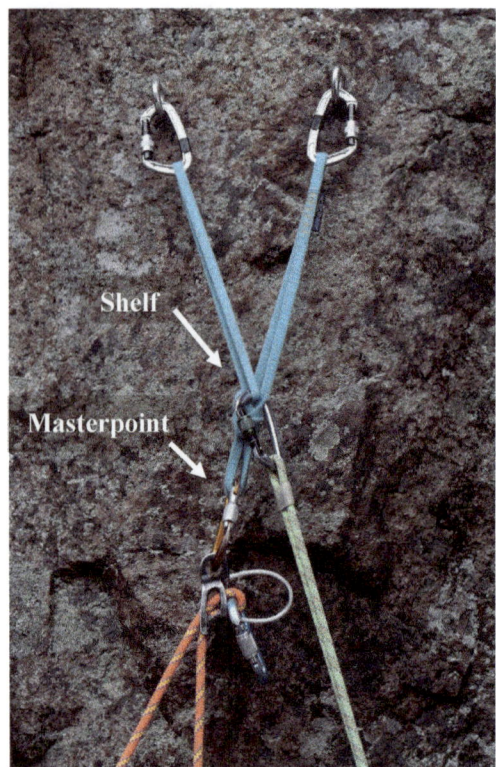

Pre-equalised belay anchor

If the shelf is clipped, but without anything clipped to the masterpoint, if the anchor knot were to untie, the shelf would disappear. Therefore, even if the masterpoint is not being used, always keep a locking carabiner clipped to it to maintain the integrity of the shelf.

The quad

The quad, yet another two-point anchor rig, is useful as it provides not only two independent masterpoints (although no shelf) but is also self-equalising. Whereas with a classic pre-equalised anchor, the masterpoint knot must be untied and retied at each belay station, the knots used in the quad can be left in the sling from pitch to pitch. (Be sure to unknot the sling at the end of the day so that the knots don't become permanent.) This will help to speed up the belay transitions on a long route requiring efficiency.

The quad is best tied using a 240cm sling (or equivalent cordelette). Start by doubling the sling, clip it into one anchor point, tie two overhand knots to make the sling redundant (and limit extension), then clip the second anchor point. Each masterpoint consists of any two of the four strands.

The quad belay anchor

A note on clipping into the belay anchor

The simplest way to clip into a belay anchor is with your personal tether. As explained in previous chapters, it is important to use a dynamic tether and not a static sling. Although a sling provides more than enough strength, shock loading a static system will generate huge forces that could injure the climber and compromise the gear. Even when clipped into the belay anchor with a dynamic tether, you should be careful to position yourself such that your tether is always under tension to prevent any possibility of a shock load. At times, you may wish to be positioned either closer to or further away from the belay anchor. Since a personal tether is not adjustable, it can be practical to instead use the climbing rope to clip yourself into the anchor directly using a clove hitch on a locking carabiner. This allows you to reposition yourself and adjust the length of rope, all the while remaining safe (note that to adjust a clove hitch you must first take your weight off it).

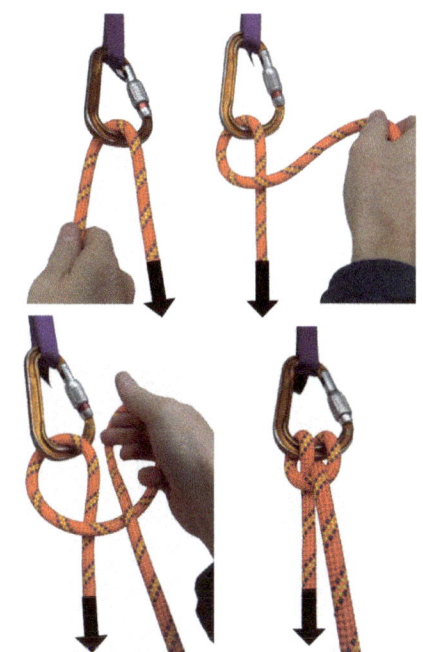

Tying a clove hitch with one hand. Arrows point towards the harness tie-in knot.

Using the climbing rope to clip in directly to the masterpoint of a belay anchor with a clove hitch

To tie a clove hitch with one hand, start by clipping the rope as for clipping a quickdraw, pull the back strand out around the first, fold the rope over to create a loop, then clip it into the carabiner. Note that twisting the loop in the wrong direction will result in a munter hitch and not a clove hitch. To verify that it's tied correctly, snug the hitch tight before trusting your life to it.

Belaying from above

After climbing a pitch, having built a belay anchor, and clipped yourself in directly, you are ready to belay up your second. There are several possible ways to belay your partner from above. Belaying directly off your harness is useful in mountaineering as a good belay stance can greatly reduce the forces experienced by a mediocre belay anchor (for example built on marginal snow pickets). Belaying with a redirect (essentially creating a mini top rope,) has the opposite result, the pulley-effect increases the force felt by the anchor. In sport climbing where bolted anchors are nearly always bomb-proof, the preferred method is to belay directly off the anchor, either with a tube device in guide mode or with an assisted-braking device like the Grigri. The advantage of belaying directly off the anchor (and not off your harness) is that you remain independent from the belay chain which makes escaping the belay simple in a rescue situation.

MULTI-PITCH SPORT CLIMBING

Tube device in guide mode

Thread your ATC as usual and clip the rope and cable with a locking carabiner, but then with another locking carabiner, clip the second attachment on the device either to the masterpoint or the shelf of the belay anchor. (Always read the instructional booklet that comes with your belay device.)

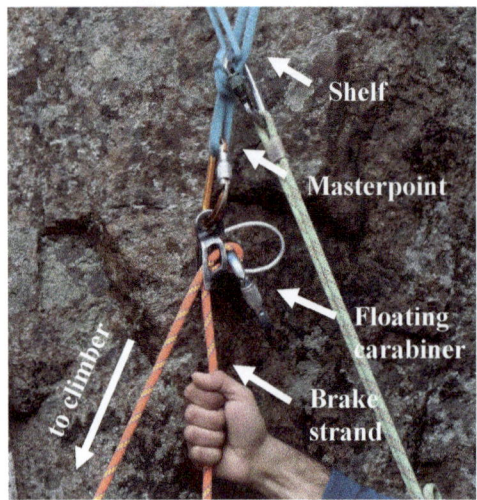

Belaying off the anchor with a tube device in guide mode

Whereas you can easily pull slack through the device, when the climber's strand is weighted, the two ropes running in opposite directions create enough friction to hold the climber's fall. Despite its auto-locking function, always keep a hand on the brake end of the rope. Although tube devices in guide mode are very convenient in taking up slack, the auto-locking feature make it difficult to pay out rope to your second.

Giving slack with a tube device in guide mode

To pay out slack without letting go of the brake end of the rope, first slide your brake hand down the rope and use your thumb to lift the floating carabiner of the belay device, then with the other hand, pull slack through the system.

To lower the climber, see "lowering the second with a tube device in guide mode" in Chapter 6.

Grigri

The Petzl Grigri is an assisted-braking belay device popular with sport climbers and can be used to belay a second from above. However, since you can't rappel with a Grigri, it is less suited for multi-pitch climbing. To belay a second with a Grigri, simply clip the device to either the masterpoint or shelf of the belay anchor. Make sure to position the device so the braking cam is oriented away from the rock and can freely move. As for belaying a leader, always keep a hand on the brake end of the rope.

MULTI-PITCH SPORT CLIMBING

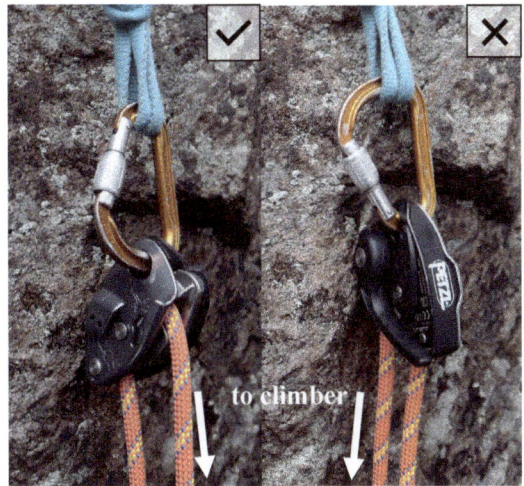

Belaying off the anchor with a camming assisted-braking belay device. Make sure to position the device with the cam oriented outwards.

If the Grigri is oriented in a way such that the cam is pressed up against the wall, the rock could prevent the camming mechanism from engaging.

Munter hitch (aka. Italian hitch)

The munter hitch is similar to the clove hitch but with one less twist. It is a friction hitch that can be used to belay either the leader or the second, or to descend on rappel. In the event that you drop your belay device, this hitch will prove to be very useful. As we will see, a munter hitch is essential in many rescue situations. Although a munter hitch is not auto-locking, it provides the necessary friction to catch a fall. The disadvantage of using a munter under tension (to lower or rappel) is that it twists the rope.

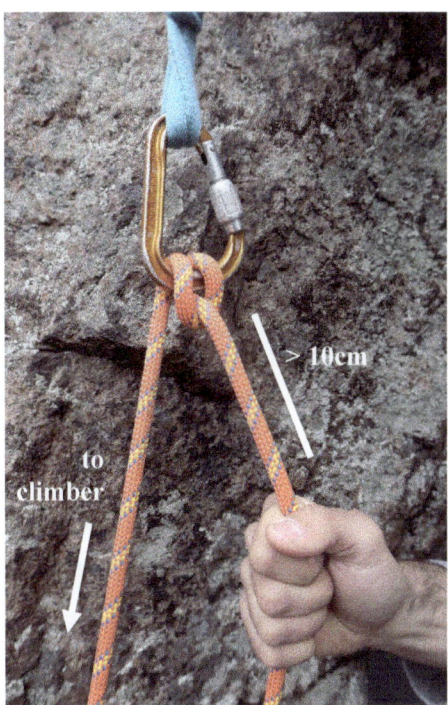

Belaying off the anchor with a munter hitch

A munter hitch works best when tied on an HMS (pear-shaped) carabiner.

*A munter hitch is NOT auto-locking, and one must always remain in total control of the brake end of the rope. Because the hitch will flip in its orientation in the event of a fall, always hold the break strand at least 10cm from the hitch so as not to pinch your hand in the carabiner.

The monster munter

To tie a monster munter begin with a munter hitch, then wrap the climber's end of the rope behind the brake stand and clip it back into the carabiner.

MULTI-PITCH SPORT CLIMBING

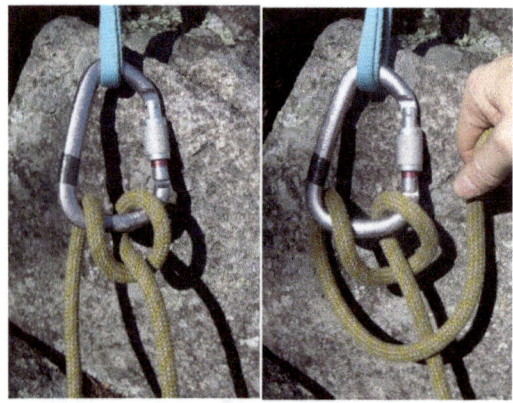

This essentially creates a second munter hitch around the first and in doing so, twists the rope in the opposite direction. The result is a hitch with more friction than a simple munter, that doesn't twist the rope nearly as much (it twists the rope at two points in opposite directions). Although overkill in most situations, this hitch can be useful when the load is heavy or the rope skinny.

The monster munter

Belaying off a natural anchor set back from cliff edge

After topping out, you may find the belay to be on a tree instead of bolts. Although simple in principle, the fact that a good tree is often set well back from cliff edge complicates things. To facilitate communication and reduce rope drag, it is preferable to belay at cliff edge and not 10m back somewhere in the forest as this would make friction unreasonable and communication impossible. First build a belay anchor on the tree. You then need to extend the anchor using the climbing rope to position yourself at cliff edge. Pull up more than enough slack, anchor the rope to the masterpoint using a figure-of-8 on a bight, then clip yourself in with a clove hitch on your belay loop. This way you can easily adjust the length of the rope to position yourself at exactly the desired spot. In this situation, it is still possible to belay directly off the anchor (ATC clipped to the tree in guide mode), although giving slack would be long and tedious if the belay device is out of reach. This set-up would be acceptable if the terrain facilitated quick and safe travel between the belay anchor and cliff edge.

Belaying off the anchor

Alternatively, you could belay directly off your harness, (with the ATC clipped to your belay loop). This is the fastest system to set up, but being a part of the belay chain complicates matters significantly if you ever need to escape the belay.

Belaying the second directly off the harness with an ATC. Be sure that the belayer is positioned on the line created between the belay anchor and the direction of pull in the event of a fall.

If belaying the second directly off your harness, using the ATC in guide mode will provide more security and is generally a good idea, especially if you think your second may need to be taken tight and hang on the rope.

Belaying the second directly off the harness with and ATC in guide mode

Although longer to set up, the best technique is to belay off of an alpine butterfly knot tied in the climbing rope, within arm's reach, between the belayer's clove hitch and the belay anchor. This keeps the belay device within arm's reach and the belayer independent from the belay chain. If the rope extension is considered part of the belay anchor, then this essentially creates an extended masterpoint to belay off of.

In review, to build an extended belay anchor, first build a redundant anchor on the tree. Pull up more than enough slack and anchor the rope to the tree with a figure-of-8 on a bight. Attach yourself to the rope with a clove hitch on your belay loop then reposition yourself near cliff edge, adjusting the hitch as necessary. Tie an alpine butterfly knot in the climbing rope between the clove hitch and the tree anchor. Readjust the clove hitch as necessary. Belay with the ATC in guide mode clipped to the alpine butterfly knot.

Belaying off an extended anchor using an alpine butterfly as a masterpoint

The technique employed will depend on the relative importance of speed balanced with the likelihood that the second will need to hang on the

MULTI-PITCH SPORT CLIMBING

rope, be lowered or rescued. In all situations it is essential to have mastered the necessary techniques involved in escaping the belay and subsequent rescue options.

Stacking the rope

As the second ascends, the belayer must stack the rope in a way to keep it from getting tangled. If there is a ledge, simply feed the rope into a neat pile. In a hanging belay, you may choose to stack the rope over your personal tether. To keep the coils from getting tangled, start with long loops, then make them progressively shorter.

The belayer stacks the rope over their personal tether as the second ascends

If you are swinging leads, then the rope is stacked and ready to go for the next pitch. If however the top belayer is to lead the next pitch, it will be necessary to flip the coil over their partner's personal tether to make sure it is right side up. If you are planning this in advance, stack it backwards, starting with small loops and then progressively longer to prevent tangles.

Sequences, communication, transitions

Leading to belaying - sequence

1. When the leader arrives at the top of the pitch, they first build a belay anchor, clip themselves in directly using their personal tether or a clove hitch (either to the masterpoint or shelf), then call "secure".
2. The belayer should confirm this command, then detach their belay device. If there is ever any uncertainty, keep the leader on belay.
3. The leader then pulls up the remaining rope and stacks it either on a ledge or coiled over their personal tether.
4. When the rope becomes taught, the second calls "that's me" so the leader knows that they have retrieved all the slack.
5. The leader then puts the second on belay and calls "on belay".
6. The second should confirm this, then, if on the second pitch or higher, cleans the lower belay anchor, then calls "climbing" and off they go.

Note: before the leader leaves the ground, be sure that both partners tie into opposite ends of the rope. Also, make sure to have all your gear in order; anything you'll leave on the ground must be packed up, (nothing will blow away with a gust of wind, your gear will stay dry in the event of an afternoon rain, and extra food is strung on a tree to keep the critters out,) and everything you'll take up with you is close by. When your partner is pulling up the slack to put you on belay, you need to be ready to go, not looking for your shoes in a backpack 10m away in the forest. Remember that safety on a long multi-pitch route may depend on speed and efficiency.

A note on communication

If pitches are long, belay ledges inset, or if there is background noise of a river, waterfall or wind, communication can be next to impossible. In this situation it will be essential to have worked out rope-tug signals with your partner. Generally, three slow, long tugs from the leader communicates to the second that they are on belay and can climb when ready. As a belayer, when in doubt due to poor verbal communication, keep your partner on belay. If belaying the leader who you suspect to have reached the anchor, keep them on belay, even if it means paying out slack until you reach the end of the rope which is tied to you, at which point you can unclip your belay device and wait for the rope-tug signals. If belaying the second, after leading a pitch and pulling up the rope, put the second on belay as soon as possible and without hesitation. Be sure to confirm rope-tug signals with your partner beforehand.

Belay station transition - sequence

1. When the second arrives at the belay anchor, they first clip themselves directly into the anchor (masterpoint or shelf) using their personal tether or a clove hitch.
2. After communicating all intentions, the leader can take the second off belay.
3. Transfer all gear to the new leader.
4. Stack the rope if necessary.
5. Put the new leader on belay.

Swinging leads, (where partners alternate who leads and who seconds each pitch) is the most efficient tactic since the rope can be stacked by the belayer as they belay the second. If the same person is to lead two pitches in a row, it's best to re-flake the rope to avoid knotting.

Avoiding a factor two fall

The forces generated by a leader fall are the result of 3 main things: 1. the mass of the climber, 2. the elasticity of the rope/belay method employed, and 3. the fall factor. For a given climbing team, the fall factor is the most important determinant of the severity of a fall. The fall factor is calculated as the length of the fall divided by the amount of rope in the system.

$$\text{Fall Factor} = \frac{\text{Length of fall}}{\text{Amount of rope in system}}$$

For a short fall, the leader accumulates little kinetic energy, which is then absorbed primarily by the elasticity of the rope. If there is a lot of rope in the system, then there is more elasticity to absorb the energy generated by the fall (the climber will decelerate over a longer period). In this case (short fall on a lot of rope,) the fall factor is small and thus the forces felt by the climber, belayer and equipment are also small.

Conversely, a long fall on a short amount of rope creates much energy that is to be absorbed by only a small amount of rope, thus the fall factor and forces are high and the fall violent. The worst-case scenario is a factor two fall, where the climber falls twice the length of rope in the system. In multi-pitch climbing, this represents the leader falling directly onto the belay anchor before clipping the first piece of protection. A factor two fall, (also known as a "death fall,") can generate enough force to damage climbing equipment and seriously injure the climber and must be avoided at all costs. Furthermore, the downward pull on the belayer instead of the normal upward pull could be extremely painful for the belayer and cause them to lose control of the brake strand. If you are not able to easily reach the first bolt after the belay, it is good practice to clip a quickdraw directly into one of the anchor bolts as your first piece of protection. If this creates rope drag, the belayer can remove it after the climber has clipped the next bolt. Note that this may or may not be a good idea for an anchor built on trad gear as a fall on single anchor point could compromise the entire belay anchor.

A quickdraw clipped directly to the anchor prevents the possibility of a factor two fall. Note how the masterpoint is clipped with a locking carabiner to maintain the integrity of the shelf.

Climbing as a party of three

Although it is most common to climb multi-pitch routes as a party of two, climbing as a party of three can provide both company and security. There are two common methods of climbing as a party of three.

The Caterpillar

The first climber leads the pitch on a single rope. The second climber is then belayed up from above. As they climb, they unclip the first rope from the protection and reclip a second rope which they are trailing. Once at the upper belay, climber two then belays climber three up from above. Climbers can switch roles so as to share leads, however, this may necessitate redoing tie-in knots. Whoever is acting as the second climber must be tied into both ropes, one to climb on, and one to trail up for the last climber.

Simul-belaying

Climbing on two ropes and simul-belaying is much faster than the caterpillar technique but requires more attention and is potentially more dangerous. The leader will be tied into two ropes and the second and third climbers tied into the end of one each. The first climber begins by leading the pitch on two ropes. The leader should clip the two ropes alternatively into protection points. If the route is at all traversing or overhanging, the leader must be sure to clip their ropes to protect both the second and third climbers (see Chapter 7, double ropes for an in-depth explanation). Using an ATC style device in guide mode, the leader can then belay both climbers up simultaneously, one on each rope. If one climber falls, the device will lock off on one rope, but the other remains free. Always remain in control of both brake strands and pull the slack through differentially to keep both followers safe. The climbers should be staggered by at least a few meters so that one does not fall on the other.

This technique is best practised using two single-rated ropes instead of a pair of double ropes. Double ropes aren't designed to be used one at a time and their small diameter means that they can more easily be severed. However, the flip side is that leading on two single ropes may increase the impact force of a leader fall due to decreased elasticity.

MULTI-PITCH SPORT CLIMBING

Belaying two seconds simultaneously

To keep communication clear, finish each command with the rope colour. For example, a second may call "Up rope green!" or "Climbing on pink!".

Multi-pitch rappelling

If there is a descent trail, the safest and most enjoyable way to get down is often to hike. If not, getting down off a multi-pitch route will involve a series of rappels. The first consideration if planning to rappel is the location and state of the rappel anchors. In sport climbing, since belay anchors usually consist of two bolts, rappelling often involves using these same belay anchors as rappel anchors. However, if the route has long traversing sections, the rappel line may be different from the way in which you ascended. Also, if the route is popular with several parties ascending simultaneously, rappelling the route may be inconsiderate, creating a traffic jam, or even dangerous, causing loose rocks to fall on parties below. Make sure to research the route before leaving the ground.

Established rappel anchors off the bolted belay line may use a combination of natural trees, bolts, pitons and fixed trad gear. These are often linked together with webbing. It is possible for rappel anchors to be in very poor condition due to exposure to the elements. Although rappel anchors never take that much force, if they fail, they will likely result in death. Never get into the habit of using rappel anchors without first thoroughly inspecting them. If the sling looks old, cut it away and replace it with a new one. As for belay anchors, make sure they are always redundant.

At times, one 60m rope is sufficient to get you back to the ground, but often rappel/belay anchors will be bolted at up to 60m intervals, requiring two ropes to get back down. This is especially true if the rappel line is different from the climbing route. This is important information you must know before leaving the ground. If rappelling on two ropes, after passing the rope through the rappel anchor, one must tie the two ropes together. Such a knot is known as a "bend".

Bends

Which bend to use to tie two rappel ropes together is a historically contentious subject. Several fatal accidents caused by poorly tied knots have influenced the debate. Recommended bends have gone in and out of fashion as relative advantages and disadvantages of each of a number of imperfect knots are considered and reconsidered. Here we consider several options.

Several acceptable bends exist for attaching two rappel ropes together including the double fisherman's, Flemish bend and flat overhand. While some have more of a tendency than others to get stuck in cracks or become difficult to untie, all are safe options when tied correctly. The only bend shown here that must be avoided, having resulted in several accidents, is the flat figure 8 bend. The most comprehensive set of testing done on the strength of different rappel knots was done by Thomas Moyer, whose data is used below.

MULTI-PITCH SPORT CLIMBING

Double fisherman's bend

The traditional bend used to tie two rappel ropes together is the double fisherman's described in Chapter 2. Although extremely strong, the knot has the tendency to snag and get stuck in cracks when pulling the ropes down and is difficult to untie after being weighted.

Double fisherman's

Flat overhand bend (aka. "Euro death knot", EDK)

Despite its name, this once forbidden knot is safe and is actually the most commonly tied rappel knot. It has become the norm because it tends to get jammed in cracks less frequently than the double fisherman's, a potentially serious problem on multi-pitch rappels. The asymmetrical nature of this knot allows it to run smoothly over the rock without damaging the rope, makes it less prone to getting stuck and remains easy to untie after being weighted. Americans once skeptic of this seemingly simple knot's popularity in Europe gave it its morbid nickname.

Flat overhand EDK

Although the flat overhand is significantly weaker than the double fisherman's, it is sufficiently strong for most if not all rappel scenarios. Rappelling generates very low forces (body weight plus bounces) and the flat overhand tied correctly is more than sufficient. To prevent the knot from capsizing (rolling down the tails), it must be properly dressed (without crosses), snugged tight, and have long tails of at least 30cm. If tied correctly, tests have shown that it will not capsize until ~6.2 kN (630kg), more than sufficient given that the rappel knot only takes half of the total force generated by the rappel which in itself is never much more than body weight.

However, if the knot is not dressed, snugged tight, or if the tails are too short, the flat overhand can pose serious risks. An undressed and loose flat overhand will capsize under much lower forces, only ~1.1 kN (113 kg). Be extremely diligent in properly tying, dressing and setting this knot. Although some advocate for tying a second overhand to back up the first one, I argue that this defeats the purpose of using this knot to begin with as the extra bulk will increase the likelihood of it becoming stuck in cracks.

The flat overhand EDK is not the best bend to use in higher-force rappel situations such as tandem and simul rappels, or rappels with heavy haul bags. Using the much stronger double fisherman's knot will give you peace of mind.

When joining two ropes of different diameters, although the flat overhand EDK retains most of its strength, (an 8mm rope tied to an 11mm rope capsized at 5.47 kN in the Thomas Moyer tests,) it's generally recommended to use the more conservative double fisherman's bend.

Flemish bend (Reverse-traced figure-of-8)

A figure 8 knot rethreaded backwards creates another strong connection of two ropes. Similar in residual strength to the double fisherman's, it also tends to get snagged and can become difficult to untie after being weighted.

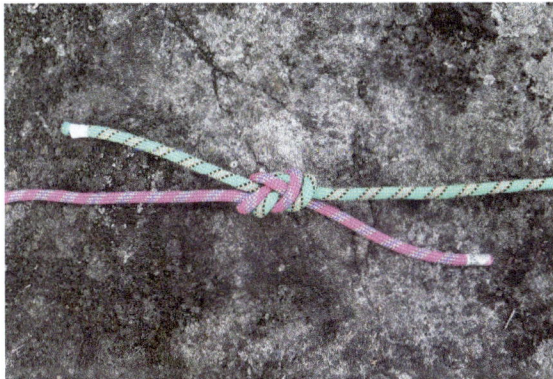
Flemish bend

This bend, while safe, is not recommended simply because of its similarity to the deadly flat figure 8 bend.

Flat Figure 8 bend (!! Danger !!)

Although loading an *overhand* knot at 180° does reduce its residual strength and decreases the force at which it will capsize, the EDK is still an acceptable bend to use for attaching two rappel ropes together. However, a similar bend using a figure-of-8 knot is dangerous, will roll under very low forces, and has been responsible for several climber deaths. **Never use a flat figure 8 bend to attach two ropes together.**

MULTI-PITCH SPORT CLIMBING

Never load a double figure-of-8 at 180°

In summary, the standard rappel knot should be the flat overhand (EDK), well-dressed, snugged down, and with sufficiently long tails. In extraordinary circumstances (two ropes of different diameters or high force rappels), the double fisherman's provides a more reliable alternative. To simplify things, always avoid all figure 8 style knots (including the Flemish bend), which will decrease the chances of tying the deadly flat figure 8 bend.

Rappel Bend	Force at which knot fails (kN)
Double fisherman's	
Dressed & tightened	12.80
Sloppy & loose	11.47
Flat Overhand EDK	
Dressed & tightened	6.22
Dressed but loose	4.76
Sloppy & loose	1.11
Flat Figure 8	
Dressed & tightened	2.62
Dressed but loose	1.29
Sloppy & loose	0.49

Thomas Moyer's 1999 data on rappel knot strength. All tests were done using 11mm dynamic climbing rope. "Knot failure" refers to the force at which the knot began to roll (capsize). If the tails weren't sufficiently long, this would result in complete failure. Otherwise, the knot would continue to roll, albeit after sequentially higher forces were applied until the knot rolled off the tails.

MULTI-PITCH SPORT CLIMBING

Multi-pitch rappel sequence using two ropes

1. Thread the rappel anchors then tie the ropes together (EDK).
2. Note which end is to be pulled later to retrieve ropes.
3. Tie stopper knots into the ends of each rope.
4. Climber one descends on rappel (with a prusik backup).
5. Once at the next rappel anchor, climber one builds an anchor and clips themselves into the masterpoint with their personal tether, frees their rappel device, then communicates ("off rappel").
6. Climber two sets up their rappel, cleans the higher anchor then rappels.
7. As climber two rappels, climber one can find the end of the rope that is to be pulled, untie the stopper knot, thread it through the next set of rappel anchors, then re-tie the stopper knot.
8. When climber two arrives at the next rappel station, they then clip into the masterpoint or shelf.
9. Before unclipping the rappel device, untie the stopper knot in the strand that is to be pulled through the above anchor.
10. Unclip the rope from the rappel device.
11. Pull the rope from the anchor above with steady movements. (Avoid sudden jerks which could result in the rope getting stuck.) Make sure the rope is attached to something so that you don't lose it. In this case, it is already threaded through the next rappel anchor.
12. After the rope falls, retie the stopper knot.
13. Center your ropes and rappel the next pitch.

Final considerations

Climbs with pitches longer than half a rope's length, traverses, overhangs, or roofs present increased risk as it may not be possible to lower the leader back to the previous belay in the event that the rock refuses passage. Before embarking on such a climb, be sure to have practiced self-rescue techniques and be confident in your ability to get down from any situation you climb into.

Essential equipment checklist

All climbing equipment must be certified by either the UIAA or CE.

- One or two dynamic single-rated climbing ropes, suggested length 60m, diameter 9.6-10mm
- 10-12 short quickdraws
- 1-2 long quickdraws
- Anchor gear (120cm or 240cm sewn sling & 2 locking carabiners) x 2
- Two quicklinks (UIAA certified)
- Dynamic personal tether
- Prusik loop (1.5m of 6 or 7mm cordelette)
- 6m of 7mm cordelette (for rescue)
- Personal locking carabiners x 5 (2 for belay device, 1 each for personal tether, prusik and long cordelette)
- Knife
- Climbing helmet
- Tube-style belay/rappel device
- Assisted-braking belay device (optional)
- Harness
- Shoes
- Chalk bag
- A friend

Become the sky
take an axe to the prison wall
escape
walk out like someone
suddenly born into colour
do it now

-Rumi

Chapter 6 – Self-rescue

Climbing is inherently dangerous and the decisions we make to mitigate the risks are based on constant risk-assessment. Risk is evaluated based on two parameters, the likelihood of an accident occurring, and the consequences of such an accident. This second parameter is highly dependent on the ability as a climbing team to quickly and efficiently get back to the ground in a safe and autonomous manor. For example, if a party doesn't have the skills necessary to rescue an injured partner off a traversing section of a multi-pitch route, then embarking on a such a pitch where there is even a remote possibility of a fall increases risk dramatically. Calling the authorities for help to get off a route may be an option in certain regions but may be unfeasible or impossible for others. It is your responsibility to be aware of rescue services offered in the regions where you climb and carry relevant phone numbers. Although calling in a professional rope-rescue may be an option in serious situations, it may be less than an ideal option due to the increased exposure or worsening of untreated injuries associated with the wait, not to mention the potentially crippling price tag.

Self-rescue often refers to a series of rope tricks needed to get you and your partner safely off a climb (either up or down) in the event of an unplanned mishap or accident. However, these self-rescue techniques are most often employed not as a result of a serious accident, but rather to avoid one. For example, without the knowledge of either ascending a rope with prusiks or a mechanical advantage ascension rig, a situation where the second simply isn't able to pull past a crux move near the top of a multi-pitch climb as the sun is setting or a storm is brewing can become a serious situation without any unexpected accident besides the route being harder than expected.

A mastering of all skills necessary to get out of any situation that you chose to climb into is an essential part of gaining autonomy as a rock climber and should be practiced regularly. Besides the rope tricks necessary to get off a route, climbers, (especially those who climb long multi-pitch routes or in remote locations) should have a basic knowledge in wilderness first aid in order to stabilize an injured partner, and a plan to get from the bottom (or top) of a route to the nearest hospital (or at least the local pub).

Basics

The best way to stay safe climbing is to make good decisions that will prevent the need for self-rescue. Since all climbing safety is based on risk assessment and mitigation, it is of course impossible to make an exhaustive list of rules to follow. However, consider the following tips to reduce risk:

- Choose reliable and safe climbing partners
- Use equipment that's in good condition
- Wear a helmet
- Use simple and clear communication
- Always respect the rule of redundancy
- Always do a partner check before climbing
- Always check your safety set-up before calling "secure" or unclipping your personal tether from an anchor (to rappel, lead the next pitch, etc.)
- Avoid areas with loose rock
- Keep the rope away from sharp rock
- Inspect all anchors before using them, especially established rappel anchors built using slings or cordelette
- Always rappel with a prusik backup and stopper knots in the ends of both ropes
- Always knot the other end of the rope (stopper knot, or the belayer's tie-in knot) before leading a pitch
- Climb in control

SELF-RESCUE

- Choose routes within your ability
- Always carry appropriate gear for the climb, including self-rescue gear
- Don't hesitate to bail if your instincts are telling you to
- Research routes, approaches, and descents beforehand
- Be careful not to climb off route
- Be conservative in planning your time on multi-pitch routes
- Use proper judgement and trust your instincts

However, at times you may find yourself in a pickle requiring self-rescue skills. Before hastily tying complicated knots, climbing ropes and cutting others, first take a deep breath and thoroughly assess the situation, then make a logical plan and retrieve the necessary gear before finally starting to carry it out.

Never put yourself in danger; rescuing two victims is harder than rescuing one. As in all climbing situations, make sure to respect the rule of redundancy. The only non-redundant parts of the system should be:

1. The climbing rope
2. Your dynamic personal tether, and its locking carabiner
3. Your belay/rappel device, its locking carabiner and the harness belay loop

*Never trust your life to a single prusik

<u>Essential gear to have at all times</u>

Rescue equipment to be carried at all times by each partner include:

- prusik "rescue loop" (1.5m of 7mm cordelette tied in a loop with a double fisherman's)
- 6m of 7mm cordelette*
- 2 locking carabiners, one of which is pear-shaped
- knife
- minimal first-aid supplies should include tape, pain killers, and something to stop excessive bleeding and dress wounds with

Instead of a 6m strand of cordelette, some climbers prefer to carry a second short rescue loop which can be used analogously.

Friction hitches

Friction hitches are used to anchor a smaller diameter cordelette to a larger diameter climbing rope. When weighted, the friction hitch bites into the rope and holds, but can slide along it when unweighted. Although the prusik is the most common and reliable friction hitch, several others exist that can be useful in specific circumstances. For all of the following hitches, friction is increased by adding more wraps or by increasing the difference between diameters of the two ropes. In order to be full strength, 7mm cordelette is recommended. Smaller diameter cordelette will create more friction but aren't strong enough to be reliable in most rescue situations.

<u>Prusik</u>

The prusik is the most secure friction hitch, offering the greatest holding power with a minimum of three wraps.

SELF-RESCUE

A three-wrap prusik

Klemheist

The Klemheist is similar to the prusik, but is asymmetrical, generating significant friction in only one direction. This makes it ideal for ascending a fixed rope as it is easier to slide upwards. The Klemheist is also the preferred hitch to tie if using a nylon sling instead of cordelette.

Klemheist

Autoblock ("French prusik")

The autoblock (sometimes called the "French prusik") offers the least amount of friction but is fast and easy to tie. It is often used to back up a rappel, but it should not be used for rescue applications where it is holding the entire load of the climber. Subsequent wraps can quickly shorten the cord and generate more friction.

Autoblock

Catastrophe knots

A catastrophe knot is a general term for a backup knot. It never takes weight *a priori*, but if everything else were to fail, it would prevent a catastrophe. Most often tied as an overhand or figure 8 on a bight, depending on the situation it may be tied in either a single strand or double strand (sometimes called BFK, or Big Friggin' Knot), may be then clipped to a belay anchor, your belay loop, or simply serve as a mid-rope stopper knot to prevent the rope(s) slipping through a belay or rappel device. If it is important to keep the backup adjustable, a clove hitch tied on a locking carabiner can be used as an alternative to the overhand.

SELF-RESCUE

A catastrophe knot (overhand on a bight) on two strands used to back up a rappel

Getting hands free

The first step in nearly all rescue situations is to get hands free. If belaying with an ATC off your harness, the preferred method to tie off your belay device is with a mule knot backed up with an overhand.

Mule-Overhand (MO) tied on a tube belay device

First, while maintaining tension, pass the brake end of the rope through the belay carabiner, then tie a mule knot.

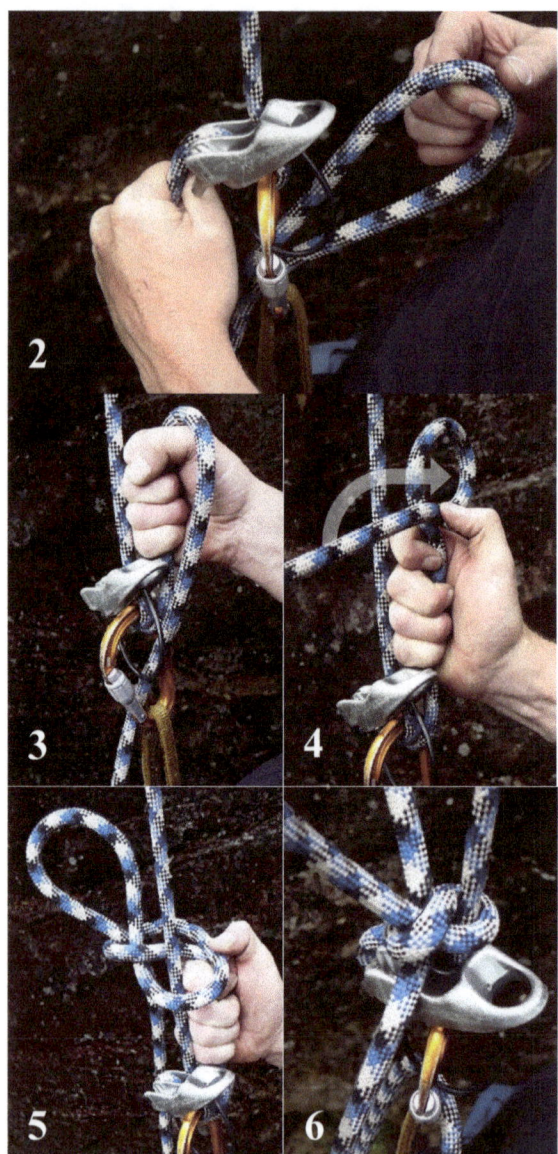

Tying a mule knot on a tube belay device

Finally, using the loop created by the mule knot, tie an overhand around the climber's strand of the rope to back up the mule knot.

SELF-RESCUE

Munter hitch

A MO tied on an ATC

Throughout the first half of the sequence (until the mule knot is completed), be sure to have at least one hand in total control of the brake end of the rope.

Munter-Mule-Overhand (MMO)

A mule-overhand is also used to tie off a munter hitch. The following combination of knots and hitches is referred to as a "MMO."

Before tying off the munter hitch with a mule-overhand, if not already under tension (as will be the case when tying a PMMO) be sure it is flipped into the corrected orientation to hold the

SELF-RESCUE

load. If this doesn't make sense, play around with a munter hitch and you'll immediately notice how it flips between two different orientations depending on which strand is loaded.

Tying off a munter hitch with a mule-overhand

A completed MMO

Tube device in guide mode

If you are belaying your second directly off the anchor with a tube device in guide mode or a mechanical device like a Grigri, getting hands free is as simple as tying an overhand on a bight in the brake end of the rope as a backup knot.

Escaping the Belay

Once your belay device is tied off, you may need to escape the belay. If belaying the second directly off the anchor, you are not a part of the belay chain to begin with. If belaying off your harness (ex. belaying the leader) you will need to transfer the climber's weight off of your belay device and onto a prusik holding the rope and attached to the anchor to enable you to get out of

SELF-RESCUE

the system. This may be necessary in order to go get help, or to free yourself in order to carry out the next step of the rescue (ex. ascend to the leader or rappel to the second).

Prusik-Munter-Mule-Overhand (PMMO) using a cordelette

The PMMO is a series of knots and hitches that creates a prusik that is releasable. By this I mean that weight can be transferred onto the prusik, but also, weight can be released from the prusik (by undoing the mule-overhand) and transferred onto another component of the system. Any time a PMMO or MMO is used in the following example, it is to keep the system releasable.

A completed PMMO tied on two strands of cordelette

Although 6m of 7mm cordelette is best for rigging a PMMO, some climbers will instead choose to carry a second short rescue loop. The prusik can then be made releasable using the climbing rope. First tie a prusik with a short rescue loop, then use the standing end (other extremity) of the climbing rope to tie a MMO to the carabiner of the rescue loop.

PMMO tied with a short rescue loop and the standing end of the climbing rope

Escaping the belay - sequence

Step 1: If not already belaying from an anchor (ex. top rope, single-pitch lead), it will be necessary to first locate where you will build the anchor onto which you will transfer the climber's weight. This will likely be the closest tree. If belaying the leader on a multi-pitch route, you'll use the anchor you're clipped to.

107

SELF-RESCUE

Step 2: Get hands free – tie off the ATC using a Mule-Overhand (MO), or if belaying with a Grigri, with an overhand on a bight in the brake strand.

Step 3: If necessary, construct an anchor. If you're on a trad anchor, it may be necessary to reinforce it to hold an upward pull. If on the ground, the easiest way to build a tree anchor, using the least amount of gear, is with the climbing rope itself. Locate the end of the rope, tie a figure-of-8, wrap the tree (more than once so the rope doesn't slip upwards), then complete a figure 8 follow-through. Finally, tie another figure-of-8 on a bight to act as a masterpoint.

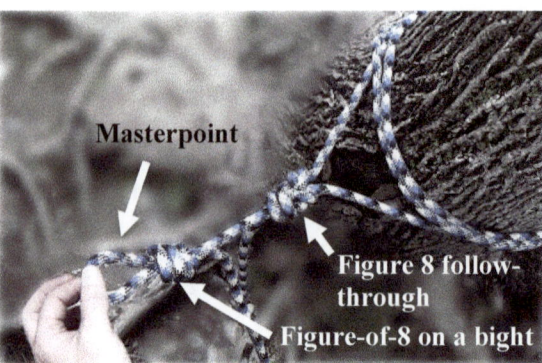

Step 4: Using a long cordelette, place a prusik hitch on the climber's strand of the rope.

Step 5: Attach the other end of the cordelette to the anchor's masterpoint using a MMO (munter-mule-overhand) on a locking carabiner to create a PMMO. First set the munter hitch, be sure that it is flipped into the lowering position, then tie it off with a mule-overhand.

SELF-RESCUE

Step 6: Push the prusik up so there is no slack in the system.

Step 7: Transfer the climber's weight directly onto the anchor via the PMMO. First undo the mule-overhand on your belay device, then give slack until the prusik engages.

Note: Do not detach your belay device. You should never completely rely on a prusik as the only point of attachment.

Step 8: Before removing your belay device, tie a munter hitch with the brake end of the rope onto a locking carabiner clipped directly to the anchor masterpoint.

Note: To maintain redundancy, never let go of the brake strand during this process

Step 9: Maintaining control of the brake end of the rope (after the munter) remove your belay device. Then pull out all the slack (maintaining the munter hitch flipped in its correct orientation) and tie off your munter hitch using a mule-overhand.

109

SELF-RESCUE

Step 10: Since you may need your long prusik cordelette later in the rescue, (for example to climb

the rope,) you may want to retrieve it. Untie the mule-overhand of the prusik cordelette and transfer the weight from the PMMO onto the MMO tied in the climbing rope.

Step 11: Remove the prusik cordelette entirely.

Rescuing yourself

If you fall off an overhanging or traversing route (as either the leader or the second), you may find yourself suspended either in mid-air or on a section of unclimbable blank rock and will need to know how to ascend your rope to get back to the route.

Ascending the rope with two prusiks

Several techniques exist to ascend a rope depending on the gear you may have, but the most basic is with two prusiks. With one prusik clipped to the belay loop and the other used as a foot ladder, like an inch worm, you work your way up the rope, weighting one prusik while sliding the other up, then vice-versa. Regardless of the set-up used, it is essential that you always remain attached to the rope with more than just one prusik.

Tie your short rescue loop to the rope with a prusik hitch and clip this to your belay loop with a locking carabiner. Just underneath, tie a second prusik to the rope for your foot ladder, (this can be with a second rescue loop, a longer 6m cordelette, or as described later, even a nylon sling). A short rescue loop used for a foot ladder will need to be extended and can be done so with a 60cm sling, clipped or girth-hitched to the rescue loop. Conversely, a 6m cordelette used as a foot ladder will need to be shortened. The length of the cordelette or sling can be further shortened by wrapping it around your foot.

It is important to back up this system so that you remain attached to the rope via more than just one prusik. The best way to do this is with a catastrophe knot on your belay loop. As slack accumulates beneath you, clip the rope directly into your belay loop with a clove hitch. This way, in case your prusiks slip or the cordelette fails, you are backed up. As you ascend, adjust the clove hitch from time to time to remove the slack.

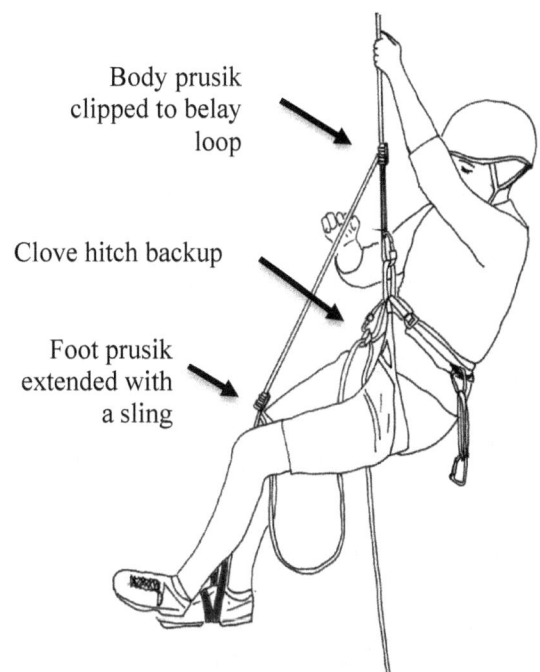

Ascending a rope with two prusiks

To ascend, first sit back on your upper prusik and slide the lower prusik up the rope. Next, stand up in your foot ladder, and holding the climbing rope, slide your upper prusik up as high as possible. The efficiency of your ascension will depend on the relative lengths of your two prusiks as well as your height. A longer body prusik requires a longer foot ladder. You want to maximize the distance you ascend with each movement. Experiment with your set-up to determine the best lengths for your body and cordage.

Another situation that may require ascension is to rescue an injured lead climber. After escaping the belay, you may need to ascend the rope to assist the leader and administer first-aid. Since the rope will likely be fixed to the lower belay anchor, the tension will make it impossible to tie a backup clove hitch in the rope. Here it is then critical to be clipped into both prusiks. You can clip into the foot ladder prusik with an extra sling or

SELF-RESCUE

your personal tether. If your foot ladder is tied with a 6m cordelette, you have more options. After tying the prusik, tie an overhand knot in the cordelette directly underneath. The overhand makes the two strands independent while conserving the integrity of the prusik hitch. Next double the cordelette back on itself and tie a big overhand knot to create two foot stirrups.

A foot ladder made from 6m of cordelette

To attach yourself to the foot prusik, you can either clip one strand of the cordelette between the prusik hitch and the overhand, or you can use the short extra loop of the foot ladder as a point of attachment. Many variations exist. Again, the rule is to never trust your life to a single prusik.

Friction hitches using nylon slings

If you are missing a cordelette or second rescue loop, you can improvise a foot ladder prusik using a 60 or 120cm nylon sling. However, avoid tying prusiks using Dyneema slings due to the slippery texture and low melting point of this material. Although in most situations, the prusik is the most reliable friction hitch, when using a nylon sling, the Klemheist tends to bight better.

Klemheist tied with a nylon sling

Ascending the rope with a prusik and a Grigri

Ascending a rope can be made much more efficient with the use of mechanical devices. Although a party is unlikely to carry mechanical ascenders, (used primarily for aid and bigwall climbing), it is possible they may have an assisted-braking belay device like the Petzl Grigri.

To use a Grigri to ascend, it will replace the short prusik (rescue loop) in the ascension rig. If you are hanging on the end of the rope, begin by tying a long prusik onto the rope as a foot ladder (this could be a double-length sling clipped to short rescue loop), step into it to create slack, then rig the Grigri underneath the prusik and clip it to your belay loop. As for ascending with two prusiks, alternate between hanging on the Grigri while sliding up the prusik and stepping into the foot ladder while pulling the slack through the Grigri. Note that the order of the two friction hitches/devices are backwards from when ascending with two prusiks (with two prusiks, the foot prusik is below the body prusik). If you are to let go of the brake strand, be sure to tie a catastrophe knot (overhand on a bight). The length of the foot ladder can easily be adjusted by wrapping the sling around your foot.

Ascending a rope with one prusik and a Grigri. Note that a backup knot (overhand on a bight) is tied in the brake end of the rope.

Likewise, an ATC in guide mode clipped to the belay loop can be used in place of a Grigri to ascend a rope in the same way.

The Garda hitch (aka. alpine clutch)

The Garda hitch is a one-way ratchet that, like a Grigri or ATC in guide mode, allows rope to slide through in one direction, but locks off if the other strand is loaded. Extremely simple, it requires only two carabiners. This hitch may come in handy to replace a Grigri if for whatever reason you find yourself in a situation where you need to ascend a rope and you only have a single prusik. The two carabiners must be identical and oriented with their gates in the same direction. Non-locking carabiners work best since the smaller profile gates will allow the carabiners to pinch against each other more tightly and block the rope. Since the rope is always pinched around the spine of the carabiners, the chance that the rope unclips is extremely low. Start by clipping the rope through both carabiners. Wrap the outer strand around the back and clip only the inner carabiner.

Tying a Garda hitch

To test the hitch, pull each strand one at a time. The rope should run freely in one direction and lock in the other. Always back up a Garda hitch (with a catastrophe knot clipped to your belay loop in this case) since its locking abilities vary with carabiner shape and are significantly less reliable than a proper assisted-braking belay device.

Bailing off a pitch above half a rope's length

Lowering off of a route requires a rope twice the length as the climber is high. In other words, with a 60m rope, you can only lower off from a maximum of 30m up. However, since it is nature who decides cliff height and belay ledge location, some routes or pitches may exceed the 30m limit. Once you've climbed higher than half of your rope's length, you'll need to have a second rope to get down.

If you need to bail off a route higher than 30m and you only have a single rope, you have only limited and imperfect options:

1. You could downclimb until 30m and then have your belayer lower you
2. If only a few meters short, you could have your belayer lower you to the end of the

SELF-RESCUE

rope (make sure there is a stopper knot to jam into the device), and then be lifted into the air to let you down to the ground after which they then downclimb the first few moves of the pitch while you spot them
3. You could fix your rope and rappel on a single strand (but you'll lose your rope)
4. You could improvise a multi-pitch rappel, but you'll have to build and leave a second rappel anchor (for trad you'll have to leave two anchors worth of gear, for sport you'll be forced to use a single bolt as your second rappel anchor unless you can find a creative way to attach two bolts together)

If you plan on climbing a pitch (either single or multi-pitch) that is longer than half a rope's length, you should carry up a second rope to get back down. This may be of significantly smaller diameter than your lead line in order to save weight and is sometimes called a tag line. However, using a full-strength single-rated rope means that it can double as an alternate lead rope if your main rope gets damaged. The second line is trailed by the leader, clipped to their harness haul loop, (where some climbers often clip their chalk bag). If you can't pass a move and need to bail before the top but after the halfway mark of your rope, you'll need to find a way to tie the two ropes together and set up a rappel to get down. Note that throughout this sequence, as always, it is best to always avoid hanging your life from a single bolt. Always respect the rule of redundancy.

1. First clip yourself in directly to the highest bolt using your personal tether.
2. Replace the quickdraw with a quicklink you'll lower off of and leave behind.
3. Call "take", unclip your tether, and have your belayer lower you to your second highest bolt.
4. Clip into the bolt with your personal tether.
5. Replace this quickdraw with a second quicklink or locking carabiner that you'll leave behind as a second anchor point.
6. Ask your belayer for slack, pull up a few meters of your lead rope from below the second highest bolt and clip this into your belay loop with a figure-of-8 on a bight as a backup catastrophe knot. Be sure your belayer keeps you on belay.
7. Also pull down some rope from above your tie-in knot, tie a knot and clip this to you temporarily to prevent the rope from pulling though the top bolt
8. Untie your tie-in knot
9. Pull up a few meters of your second line, tie a knot and temporarily clip it to something so as not to drop it
10. Untie the end of your second line from your harness haul loop
11. Tie the ends of your two ropes together. (If they are of different diameters, the best knot to use is a double fisherman's.)
12. Untie the temporary knots in the lead line and second line, but keep the catastrophe knot clipped to your belay loop as a backup (remember you're still on belay)
13. Set up your rappel on both ropes, underneath the double fisherman's bend
14. Once your rappel is set up, you can untie your catastrophe knot and have your belayer take you off belay
15. Unclip your tether, then rappel, cleaning your quickdraws as you go

Reepschnur rappel

Instead of trailing a single or double-rated climbing rope to use as a second line, some parties choose to instead carry an extremely small diameter tag line, one that is too small to actually rappel on. In this case, a Reepschnur rappel can enable a party to do a full 60m single-strand rappel on the lead line, which can then be retrieved with the small-diameter tag line. This is a useful skill to have, even if you usually climb with two single or double-rated ropes, since it can be used to rappel if one of the ropes becomes damaged.

Pass the end of the lead rope through the rappel anchors, tie a figure-of-8 on a bight in the short end, leaving a long tail, and clip this back on itself with a locking carabiner. The lead line is now essentially fixed to the rappel anchors. Tie the tag line to the tail of the lead line with an EDK or double fisherman's. You can now rappel the single strand (on an ATC or a Grigri), and once at the lower anchor, pull on the tag line to retrieve your rope.

A Reepschnur rappel setup with a small-diameter tag line (green), tied to the main line (orange) with a double fisherman's bend.

Small diameter tag lines have the tendency to become easily tangled, especially since their light weight means that a strong wind can blow them into a mess. When climbing, instead of trailing it from your haul loop, keep it neatly tied up in your backpack, and take it out only when it is to be used. A useful variation on the Reepschnur rappel to use on windy days to prevent the tag line from becoming tangled is to thread it through your rappel device along with the lead line, as though you're rappelling normally on two ropes. This keeps it in order and allows you to deal with any knotting as you rappel.

Rescuing the second

Your second hasn't made any progress in the last 10min? Can you communicate? If not, the first course of action must be to rappel down in order to assess the situation, establish communication, and then devise a plan.

Rappelling on a munter hitch

To rappel to the potentially injured (but most likely just discouraged) second, you must first tie off the belay device, fix the brake end of the rope to the belay anchor, then rappel down the single strand to establish communication (and possibly administer first aid). Since your belay device is part of the system, unless you're carrying a second, you'll need to rappel on a munter hitch, being sure to back it up with a third hand (prusik). Since you're rappelling on only one strand, it may be necessary to add an extra wrap to the prusik to increase friction, (or try the monster munter!).

SELF-RESCUE

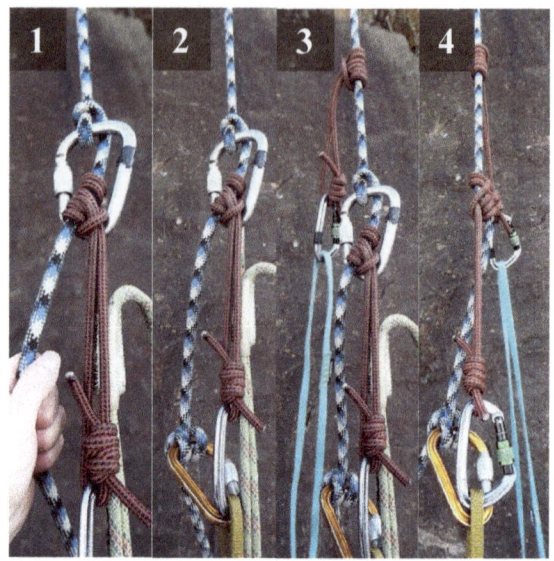

1: The brake end of the rope is fixed to the anchor with a locking carabiner clipped to the masterpoint with a figure-of-8 on a bight.

2: Rappelling a single fixed line with a munter hitch. The munter is extended on the personal tether and a third hand prusik clipped to the belay loop acts as a backup. Unfortunately, rappelling on a munter hitch will twist the rope. Try the monster munter to prevent this and to increase friction.

Converting a rappel to an ascension rig

Before rappelling, be sure you have everything you need to climb back up the rope afterwards. To convert a rappel rig into an ascension rig, you must first temporarily place a second prusik above the rappel device (in this case the munter hitch) to step into which will unweight the rappel and allow you to clean it. Be sure to tie into the rope with a catastrophe knot before cleaning the rappel to avoid relying on a single prusik. Since you'll need the catastrophe knot to be adjustable as you ascend the rope, use a clove hitch.

1: Rappelling on a munter hitch backed up with a prusik.

2: Tie a clove hitch to the brake strand as a catastrophe knot and clip this to your belay loop.

3: Add a second prusik (long cordelette or short rescue loop and sling) above the rappel munter hitch.

4: Step into the upper prusik, clean the rappel munter hitch and sit back to transfer your weight onto the lower prusik (rappel backup) still clipped to your belay loop.

SELF-RESCUE

5: Since your two prusiks are now in reverse order to ascend the rope, untie the foot prusik and retie it under the body prusik you're hanging on. You're now set up to ascend.

3:1 loop

Upon establishing communication, you may then need to then help the second ascend, lower them to the previous belay, or rescue them via a counterbalance rappel.

Helping the second up

When using mechanical advantage to help raise the second, it is best to choose the simplest system that uses the minimum advantage necessary, since too much mechanical advantage will make the raise tedious. For example, with 3:1 mechanical advantage, although you can raise 3x the weight with the same force applied to the pull strand, for every 3m you pull, the second is raised only 1m. With a 9:1 rig, you must pull 9m to raise the second just 1m.

3:1 loop

If the second is close to the belay, the simplest solution is to lower a loop of rope (the brake end of the rope) for the second to clip into their belay loop. Pulling on this creates a 3:1 mechanical advantage. This works only if the second is being belayed with an assisted-braking belay device including a tube device in guide mode.

As the belayer pulls up on the pull strand, the climber can also pull down on the inner brake strand. This is often enough to get the second past the crux.

3:1 hauling rig

If the second is further away from the belay the 3:1 Z-pulley is likely your best bet to increase mechanical advantage and help them to ascend. Tie a prusik onto the climber's end of the rope then clip the brake strand through a carabiner on the prusik. This setup creates 3:1 mechanical advantage; for each 3m you pull, the climber is lifted 1m.

SELF-RESCUE

3:1 hauling rig

Each time the rope runs through a carabiner, friction makes the system less efficient. Having one carabiner on your rack with a built-in pulley can be an incredible help.

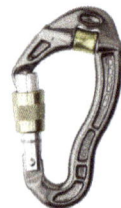

DMM carabiner with a built-in pulley

Since pulling upwards can be awkward, you can clip the pull strand of the rig through a directional clipped high on the belay anchor to change the direction of pull. However, without pulleys, this will further increase the friction in the system.

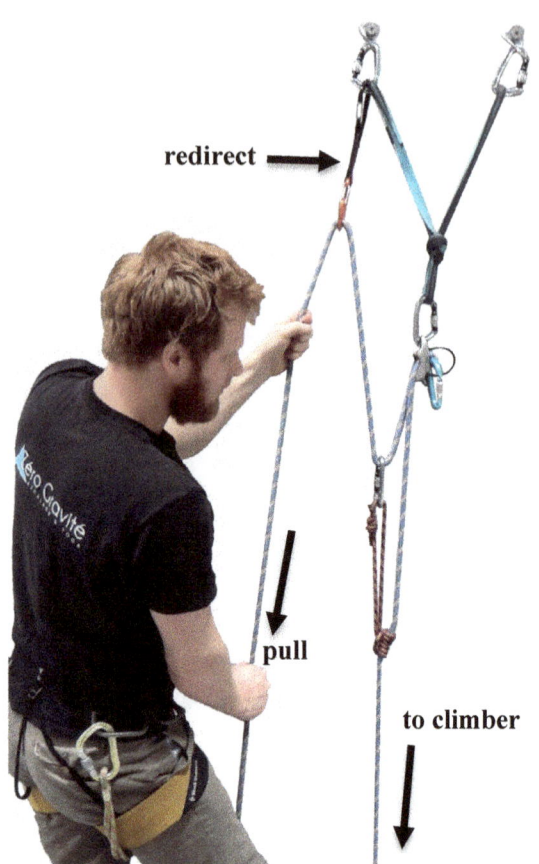

3:1 hauling rig with redirect

In all such hauling rigs, the assisted-braking belay device serves as the progress-capture pulley. Note that a camming-assisted device like the Grigri is much more efficient than a tube device in guide mode here. Not only does guide mode have increased friction, but it removes mechanical advantage from the system by only allowing the rope to be pulled when tension on the climber's strand is released, effectively turning a 3:1 into a 2:1.

Increasing mechanical advantage

If excessive friction caused by rope drag renders a 3:1 Z-pulley insufficient, it can easily be converted into a compound pulley to further increase mechanical advantage.

SELF-RESCUE

5:1 hauling rig

A 5:1 is built by inserting a simple 2:1 inside of the 3:1 Z-pulley. Instead of clipping the brake strand into the prusik, a 60 or 120cm sling fixed to the anchor acts as the internal 2:1, which the brake strand is then clipped to in order to complete the outer 3:1.

First build a 3:1 Z-pulley

A 5:1 hauling rig consisting of a simple 2:1 inside a 3:1 Z-pulley. The 2:1 consists of the yellow sling fixed to the anchor masterpoint, and the 3:1 is the Z created by the blue climbing rope. Together they create 5:1 mechanical advantage; for every 5m you pull, the climber is raised 1m.

9:1 hauling rig

Although likely overkill, mechanical advantage can be further increased by converting a 3:1 into a 9:1. This is done by simply building a second 3:1 on the pull strand of the first 3:1 Z-pulley. This then requires a second prusik.

SELF-RESCUE

A 9:1 hauling rig built by adding a second 3:1 Z-pulley onto the pull strand of the first

release hole as a lever to rotate the belay device up, gradually unlocking it. Be sure to be in <u>total control</u> of the brake strand as the belay device may unlock abruptly.

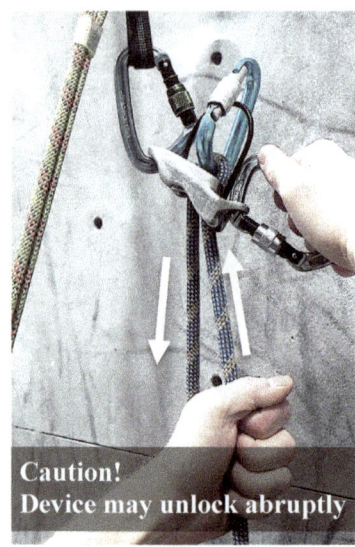

To increase friction, it is better practice to clip the brake strand of the rope through a higher redirect clipped through the shelf or an anchor point before cranking open the lever carabiner.

Once again, the pull strand can be redirected through a high point to facilitate pulling.

<u>Lowering the second with a tube device in guide mode</u>

It is not uncommon to have to lower the second, at times, all the way back to the previous belay. Although tube devices in guide mode are extremely efficient for taking in slack and locking off to hold the second, they are notoriously clumsy and potentially dangerous when used to lower the second.

If you need to lower your second only a meter or less, you can use a carabiner clipped in the

Here the brake strand is redirected through a highpoint on the anchor to increase friction

If you need to lower your second all the way down, it is best to completely disengage the belay device. A lever carabiner will not provide

120

enough force or control. Instead, the belay device can be disengaged by girth hitching a sling either through the floating carabiner or the device release hole to pull on.

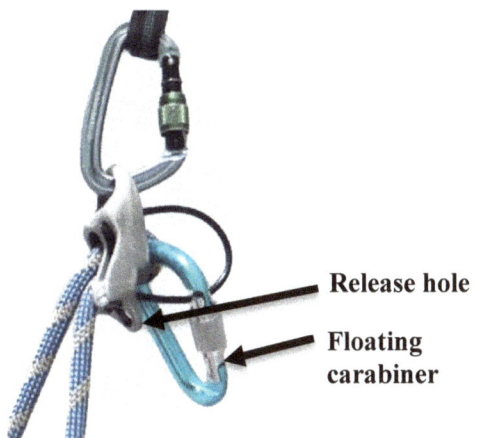

Release hole

Floating carabiner

Before you release the device, it is essential that the system is properly backed up. Here I offer two methods, one with a munter hitch on your belay loop, the other with a redirect and prusik. The first method provides more control, the second is easier to remember.

Lowering: Method 1

Step 1: Tie a MMO in the brake end of the rope to a locking carabiner clipped to your belay loop. Now you're hands free.

Step 2: Girth hitch a sling to the floating carabiner of the belay device (or through the small release hole on certain devices), then loop it through an upper point in the anchor. (Note: this can also be done using prusik cord if you're short on slings.)

SELF-RESCUE

Step 3: To disengage the belay device, either clip the sling to your belay loop and lean back or use it is a foot pedal

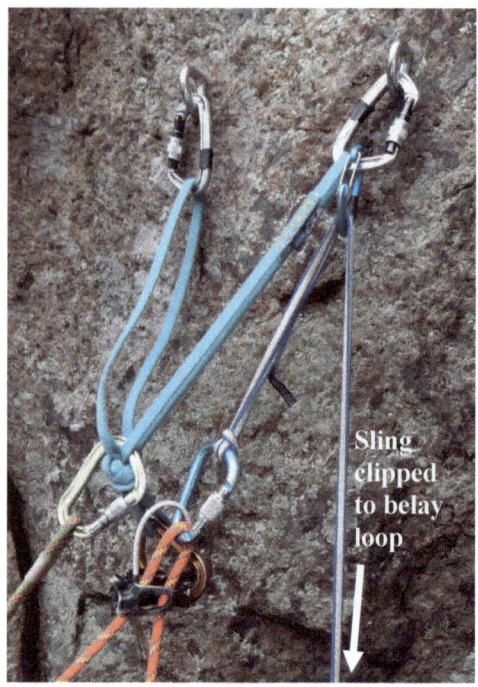

Step 4: Untie the mule-overhand and lower the second using the munter hitch.

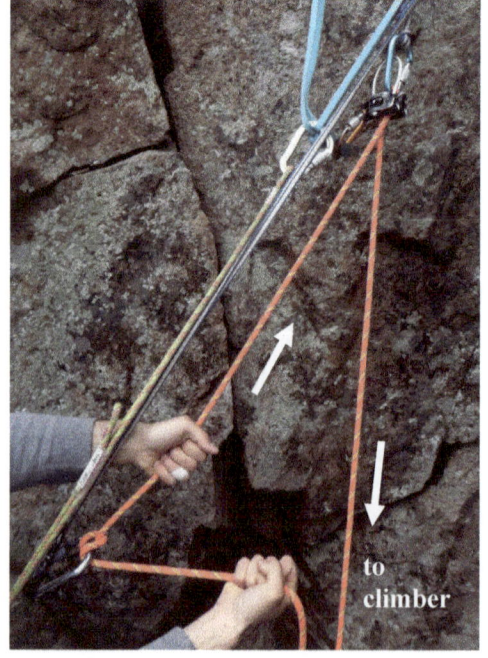

SELF-RESCUE

Lowering: Method 2

Although this alternative method offers slightly less control, it is nice in that it doesn't require the use of a MMO, a complicated knot that one forgets unless it is practised regularly. The ATC is instead backed up by two things:

- clipping the brake strand through a high redirect, and
- a prusik around the brake strand clipped to your belay loop.

Releasing an ATC in guide mode backed up with a redirect and prusik

Note that in this photo, the ATC is disengaged by a sling girth-hitched through the device release hole. The ATC can be disengaged by either stepping into the blue release sling or clipping it into your belay loop and leaning back.

Passing knots

If your rope becomes damaged during a multi-pitch climb, you can isolate the damaged section using an alpine butterfly knot.

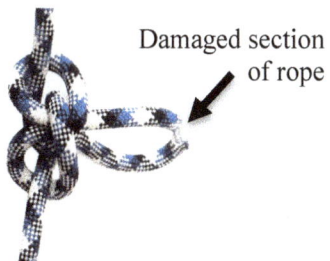

A damaged section of rope isolated with an alpine butterfly

To safely get off the route, you may need to lower your partner and/or descend on rappel. To pass a knot while lowering or on rappel, the same principles apply as when escaping the belay. As the knot approaches the belay/rappel device, the first step is to get hands free by tying off the device. Then you will transfer the weight onto a releasable prusik (PMMO) set above the knot, clipped to your belay loop. Because you should never trust your life to just one prusik, you should then tie a catastrophe knot and clip it to your belay loop with a locking carabiner. Then you can unclip the belay/rappel device and reattach it on the other side of the knot. Once again, tie off your device, then release the PMMO by undoing the mule-overhand, undo the backup catastrophe knot, release your tied-off device, and continue to lower/rappel. If after releasing the PMMO, your prusik is now out of reach and impossible to retrieve, with your device still tied off and backed up with a catastrophe knot, you can set another lower prusik that you step into, enabling you to reach higher and remove the initial prusik.

SELF-RESCUE

Compound rappels

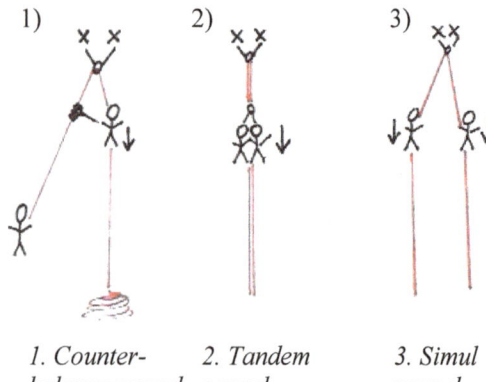

1. Counter-balance rappel
2. Tandem rappel
3. Simul rappel

Counterbalance rappel

You're belaying from above and your second is banged up, maybe unconscious, and needs to be lowered to the previous belay, but can't be lowered without your help (you need to be physically next to them to guide them down). The solution is to replace your belay device with a rappel anchor, then rappel down a single strand to your second, using them as a counterweight. Upon reaching them, you can continue down together, pulling the injured second down with a prusik attached to their strand of the rope.

Step 1: Tie off your belay device to get hands free.

Step 2: Set a prusik on the climber's strand of the rope and attach it to the anchor using a MMO to create a PMMO.

Step 3: Tie a figure-of-8 on a bight in the brake strand (if using an ATC guide or Grigri, this has already been done in step 1) as a backup catastrophe knot and clip it into the anchor with a locking carabiner.

Step 4: Give slack with your belay device to transfer the climber's weight onto the prusik. If using a tube device in guide mode, it must be opened with a sling redirected through a high point, as explained in the preceding pages.

SELF-RESCUE

pull on redirected sling to unlock belay device

Step 5: Clean the belay device and replace it with a quicklink or locking carabiner to be used as the high point of your counterbalance rappel (you will have to leave this anchor gear behind).

Rappel highpoint

Step 6: Set up your rappel rig (with a prusik backup) on the single strand.

Step 7: Remove the backup catastrophe knot clipped to the anchor.

Step 8: Weight your rappel device and tie a backup catastrophe knot in the brake strand after your third hand prusik.

To increase the friction on the single strand rappel, an extra wrap is added to the prusik

Step 9: Release the first PMMO you set, to transfer the weight of the climber onto your new anchor, held on the other side by your weight.

Step 10: Keep the long prusik from the PMMO tied on the climber's side of the rope and clip the other end of this cordelette to your belay loop to help control the climber's descent.

Step 11: Descend on rappel, sliding both prusiks down as you go.

Step 12: Upon reaching the injured second, administer first aid if necessary, then continue down using the prusik on the climber's strand to pull them down with you. The height of the prusik on the injured climber's rope will determine their position in relation to you as you descend together. It is easiest to keep the injured climber within arm's reach, just above you.

Step 13: If this doesn't get you and your partner to the ground, continue to descend the lower pitches via tandem rappel.

SELF-RESCUE

Tandem rappel

A tandem rappel is used to descend when your partner is not able to rappel autonomously. Both climbers will be clipped into the same rappel device. Clip a pear-shaped carabiner into the rope and rappel device to use as a sort of rappel masterpoint, and then clip the personal tethers of each climber to this.

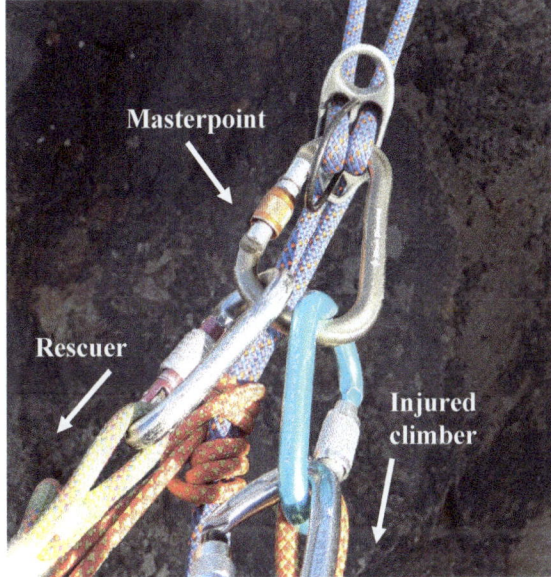

Tandem rappel set-up

Although the rappel carabiner is loaded triaxially, this trade-off is acceptable given that it is only holding body weight (x2). Note that only the rescuer has a prusik on the brake end of the ropes. Positioning yourself just beneath the injured climber helps you guide them down as you pass over uneven terrain. To set this up, clip the injured climber into the masterpoint carabiner with the short tail of their personal tether while clipping yourself in with your tether fully extended.

Chest harness

A chest harness made from a single 120cm sewn sling with a twist in the back can prove useful in keeping an injured climber upright.

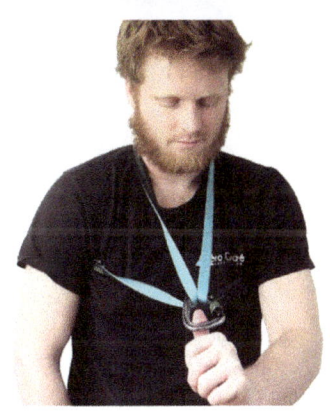

SELF-RESCUE

Alternatively, a similar chest harness can be improvised using two 60cm slings girth-hitched together. For a tandem rappel, clip the injured climber's chest harness to the carabiner of their personal tether.

Tandem rappel with chest harness

Simul rappel

A simul rappel is used as a means to get a competent party down quickly, for example in the event of an incoming storm. Both partners can rappel simultaneously, each on a single strand of the rope. If one climber is significantly heavier than the other, they should rappel on the strand opposite from the knot (if rappelling on two ropes tied together,) so that the knot prevents the ropes from slipping in the rappel anchors. If one climber unweights the rope (for example upon reaching a ledge), the other climber falls. Good communication is thus essential. Never let go of the brake strand until both you **and your partner** have arrived at the lower rappel anchor and are safely clipped in. Don't forget that you are holding not just your life but also your partner's.

Note that rappelling on a single strand generates significantly less friction than a normal rappel. Add an extra wrap to your prusik to ensure that it creates enough friction on the single strand of rope. Be especially careful if using small diameter double or twin ropes.

Rescuing the leader

If the leader is injured, in most cases, they can simply be lowered back to the belay where you can administer first aid and then continue down via tandem rappels (if not already on the ground). There are however situations where this may not be an option, for example: the route is less than vertical and lowering the leader down the slab would worsen injuries, the leader has taken a severe fall and may sustain a spinal injury, the leader fell, hit a ledge and is unconscious or otherwise helpless with their weight supported by the ledge and not the rope, the route is traversing or overhanging and so lowering the injured leader would leave them stranded far away from the belay. (In this last situation, an injured but conscious leader could likely be lowered and tossed a strand of rope that could be used to reel them back to the belay.) Similarly, in a top rope setting, the climber (likely a child) may be stuck (or convinced to be stuck) in a crack, or simply too scared to weight the rope and lower.

In these situations, it will be necessary to escape the belay and ascend the rope to assist the leader. There are two possible courses of action: counterbalance ascension or fixed-rope ascension. Counterbalance ascension refers to ascending the climber's strand acting as a counterweight on a rope that is free (not fixed to the anchor) beneath you. Fixed-rope ascension refers to ascending the climbers strand which is also fixed tight to the lower anchor.

If these maneuvers are carried out in the context of traditional climbing, significant danger is introduced as there is no guarantee that the top piece of protection (acting as the anchor as you ascend the rope) is sufficiently strong. The good news is that the piece already held the leader fall, so it should be able to also hold the additional forces generated by you climbing the rope. However, always leave a minimum of 2-3 solid pieces between the leader and you and try to keep bounces to a minimum. If in a multi-pitch context and the pitch is traversing or overhanging, be sure to keep the rope clipped to the bottom anchor, (regardless of whether you ascend in counterbalance or on a fixed line under tension) if you're wanting to make it back on the way down. The rope fixed to the anchor will guide the party back to the belay instead of rappelling into space or down a blank face.

Counterbalance ascension

Ascending to the leader without having the rope fixed to the bottom anchor.

Advantages:

- Simplest and fastest solution
- Once having reached the leader, it is simple to convert the counterbalance system into a counterbalance rappel rig

Disadvantages:

- The injured leader will certainly experience more bouncing as the second ascends. Not great if the leader has a back injury, or a member stuck in a crack.
- Potentially dangerous on a traditional route if there is any doubt in the quality of the protection.

Steps:

1. Tie off the belay device to get hands free
2. Ensure that the rope's halfway point hasn't yet passed through the belay device.
3. Set up the ascension rig (two prusiks)
4. Climb the rope (being sure to back the prusiks up with a clove hitch clipped to the belay loop) and clean the protection on the way up. Protection cleaned low on the pitch can be used higher up to reinforce the top few anchor points if necessary. Always keep a minimum of 2 bolts or 3 good gear placements between yourself and the injured leader.
5. After having reached the injured leader, convert the system into a counterbalance rappel by setting up a rappel rig on yourself, and a prusik on the leader's end of the rope to your belay loop.
6. Stabilize the leader with a chest harness if necessary
7. Descend together

A counterbalance ascension is particularly practical if the lead belayer is using an assisted-braking device such as a Grigri. The transitions from belaying to ascending to rappelling involve simply adding and then removing a single foot prusik to the rope.

If the leader has climbed higher than half of the rope's length, you will need to build an intermediate rappel anchor partway down the counterbalance rappel after which you can initiate tandem rappels.

Fixed-rope ascension

The second escapes the belay and fixes the rope before ascending.

Advantages:

- Having the rope fixed to the belay adds more security in a trad multi-pitch environment when there are few or poor-quality pieces of protection between the belay and the leader

SELF-RESCUE

- After the rope is fixed, the injured leader won't experience any movement (unless the second is significantly heavier)

Disadvantages:

- More complicated and time-consuming maneuver
- Can't be converted into a counterbalance rappel

Steps:

1. Tie off the belay to get hands free.
2. Reinforce the belay anchor to hold an upward force (not applicable if the belay is two bolts).
3. Escape the belay: transfer the climber's weight onto a releasable prusik (PMMO), then directly onto the anchor with a tied-off munter hitch (MMO).
4. Climb the rope with two prusiks (both prusiks need to be attached to your belay loop since you can't tie in backup knots when the rope below is under tension). To stay protected from below, you should leave some gear in place and simply clip it back to the rope as you pass. This is critical if there is any doubt in the quality of the top few anchor points.
5. When you reach the injured leader, build an anchor just above them (using the last two bolts on a sport climb, or with gear retrieved from the leader on a trad climb). This anchor will be left behind.
6. Clip the leader into the new anchor as tightly as possible.
7. Clip yourself into the new anchor.
8. Stabilize the leader with a chest harness if necessary
9. Either untie or cut the rope at the leader's knot to free the rope, (be sure your prusiks are well set on the line before so that you don't lose the rope).
10. With the slack, fix the rope to the new anchor.
11. Descend by tandem rappel on the single fixed line to the previous belay.
12. Clip the leader into this anchor.
13. Free the rope from the lower belay anchor and reattach it at its end, especially if the route is traversing or overhanging.
14. Ascend the single fixed rope with prusiks to your higher rescue anchor.
15. Free the rope and descend on a double-strand rappel. If the rope is not long enough to get back to the lower anchor, you'll need to build an intermediate rappel anchor partway down. If the route is overly traversing or overhanging, it may be necessary to place and abandon a couple of pieces as directionals to get you back to the belay. Alternatively, since you've attached the end of the rope to the lower belay anchor, you could likely simply reel yourself in.
16. Retrieve your rope and continue descending via tandem rappels until on the ground.

The releasable personal tether

If the injured leader is unconscious, and/or if the belays are hanging, it could be from tedious to impossible to simply unclip their personal tether from the belay anchor to initiate a tandem rappel. In such a scenario, it will be necessary to keep the system releasable at all times by clipping the injured climber into the belay anchors with a MMO in a long cordelette. This way, once the tandem rappel is set up, the climber's weight can be transferred onto it by simply releasing the MMO.

SELF-RESCUE

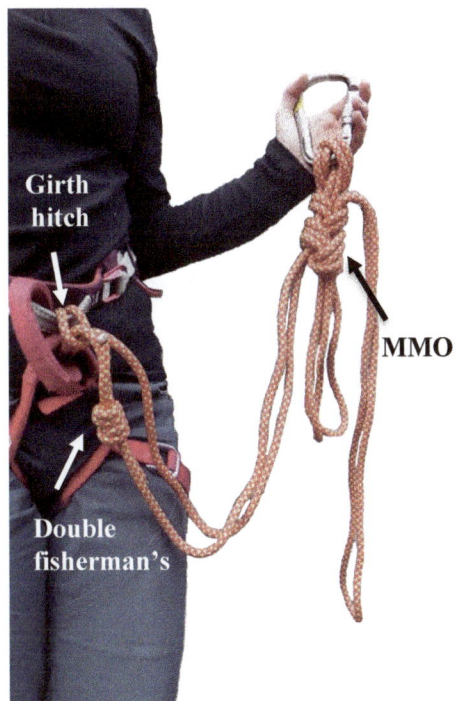

A releasable personal tether constructed from a 6m loop of cordelette

Overview of rescue sequences

Self-rescue can be broken down into two general categories: avoiding accidents and dealing with them.

Aid-climbing or ascending past an otherwise impassable section of rock, ascending the rope to regain the route after a fall and using mechanical advantage to help the second advance are all commonly used rescue techniques employed to avoid an accident.

If your partner is injured and unable to effectively retreat off a multi-pitch climb autonomously, the objective is then to gain a position to descend via tandem rappel. All of multi-pitch self-rescue can then be seen as a series of techniques to initiate a tandem rappel (except in the rare situations where it's easiest to escape the route via the top rather than the bottom).

If the injured partner is the second, the choice is then between initiating tandem rappels at either the upper belay station or the previous lower belay. If the best option is to descend, you can either lower a conscious and competent second who then builds and clips into a belay anchor where you will then join them. If the second is however not in a state to do so, you may initiate a counterbalance rappel to join the injured second and descend together to the previous belay. If it is easier to ascend to the upper belay, the injured second can either ascend the rope, or if not possible, you may use mechanical advantage to haul them up.

If the injured partner is the leader, in most situations you can simply lower them to the belay and then initiate tandem rappels. If this is not possible, the remaining solution is then to escape the belay and ascend the rope to meet and assist the leader. This can be done either in counterbalance without the rope fixed to the anchor and then converted into a counterbalance rappel to the previous belay followed by tandem rappels, or by first fixing the rope to the lower anchor, then ascending to the leader, building a new anchor and initiating tandem rappels.

Self-rescue skills can't be mastered by reading books. Get outside and practice.

SELF-RESCUE

> *Few places in this world are more dangerous than home. Fear not, therefore, to try the mountain passes. They will kill care, save you from deadly apathy, set you free, and call forth every faculty into vigorous, enthusiastic action.*
>
> **-John Muir**

Chapter 7 - Traditional climbing

"Trad climbing," (otherwise known by traditionalists simply as "climbing",) is the act of climbing without the aid of permanent bolts in the rock for protection. Practically speaking, this means that the leader must place their own protection while climbing. In line with the leave-no-trace ethic, once the climbing is done, the protection is removed, leaving the rock as it was. This way, routes are preserved for future generations in their unaltered state.

Trad climbing can be extremely rewarding as it combines adventure and mental strength with the usual physical challenges of other styles of climbing. Trad climbing can also be dangerous. The biggest hazard in rock climbing is a severe leader fall. Trad climbing increases this hazard as falls may be longer than in sport climbing due to the absence of protection or the possible failure of poor protection. Although a well-protected trad pitch can be safer than a poorly bolted sport route, not all trad pitches offer sufficient protection possibilities. As a new leader, research a route before jumping on the lead and avoid pitches with difficult protection, as well as R (runout) and X rated climbs.

In trad climbing, bad falls can become worse, or even catastrophic if poorly placed protection pulls out. Perhaps the greatest skill to possess as a trad leader is proper judgement in assessing the quality of your placements. However, since falls are uncommon and protection is rarely actually tested, it can be difficult to know how strong your protection actually is. A climber may consider themselves experienced when in reality, many of their placements are often mediocre and they are only lucky that they held during the handful of times they fell on them. Formal instruction from a guide or careful mentorship from a trusted and experienced climber are valuable aspects of the learning process.

Placing protection

The essence of trad climbing is placing protection on the lead. Being able to place solid and secure protection quickly and efficiently and then to move past with confidence is what all trad climbers strive for. However, being able to distinguish between a good and mediocre placement can be nuanced and comes only with experience. A mediocre placement can often be improved by a small adjustment. An experienced leader will be able to find the best placement possible quickly, correctly evaluate its quality, then continue accordingly.

Real learning comes from gaining experience. Before jumping on the lead, practise placing protection from the ground or while backed up with a top rope, and ask an experienced climber or guide to evaluate their quality.

Rock quality (macro and micro)

Rock protection will only be as strong as is the rock. A seemingly textbook placement of a cam that is rated to 14kN isn't very useful if it pulls out the entire detached block it was placed behind under body weight, sending the leader for a tumble and a mass of rock accelerating towards the belayer.

Rock quality must be assessed at the macro and micro levels. At the macro level, the crack must be between two massive pieces of rock. The perfect splitter crack, the "crack in the earth," runs perpendicular to the rock face, splitting the rock in two. Cracks running parallel to the rock face (behind flakes) can be extremely weak if the outer mass of rock is too thin. A piece of gear that generates outward force (like a cam) can easily pry off solid looking flakes. A splitter crack may have two solid walls, but with a thin fin or flake running

TRADITIONAL CLIMBING

parallel between the two. Avoid placing gear here. Similarly cracks between seemingly large blocks can be surprisingly weak. Unless the block is the size of a refrigerator or larger, or is pinched in place between others that are, it is likely loose and could detach enough for the piece to pull out under weight.

At the micro level, rock may change quality drastically. Otherwise good quality granite could be rotten as it exfoliates (a process somewhat like an onion shedding its skin). To test if the rock is rotten, tap it with a carabiner and listen to its sound. Similarly, a seemingly perfect splitter crack may have parts of its inner wall that are loose or flaking. In this situation, a tiny adjustment of the gear off the flake and onto the solid wall can be the difference between a bomber placement and a poor one. The inside of a crack may be uniform, or uneven from protruding pebbles, crystals or other features in the rock. Be sure that the placement isn't dependent on a micro-feature that could break under load.

Whereas a new leader (with the blessing of a thick wallet) often thinks to place only cams, lead protection can include a variety of forms depending on the route, such as trees, chockstones, threads, horns, nuts, tricams, hexes, ball nuts, big bros, pitons, and yes, cams.

Natural protection

These are gifts from nature. Before grabbing for your rack, think about if you can protect the route naturally.

Trees

A well-rooted, living tree, larger than your thigh, is a bomber anchor. Anything smaller is likely marginal. Give it a good push to assess its strength. Birch trees are weaker than they look. Since we're talking about lead protection and not a belay anchor, our criteria need not be as strict, particularly regarding redundancy. Simply sling the tree at its base with a girth hitch, clip the rope and carry on with confidence.

A tree slung with a girth hitch

Threads

Water erosion in sedimentary rock like limestone can leave tunnels that can be slung. It doesn't get much better than this.

A threaded tunnel

TRADITIONAL CLIMBING

A nut tool, usually used by the second to retrieve protection, may help you pass the sling through the tunnel.

Chockstones

A chockstone, a rock jammed into a crack, can provide a bomber anchor. Make sure to sling the chockstone such that the force doesn't rotate it out of the crack.

A slipknot

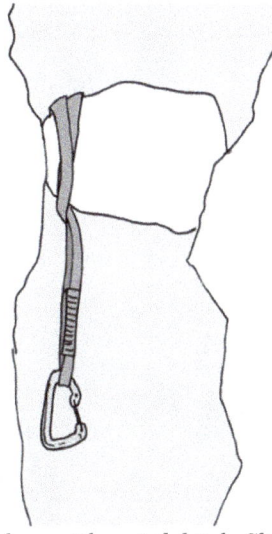

A chockstone slung with a girth hitch. Slinging it at its side as opposed to its centre will create less leverage that could potentially rotate it out of its position.

Horns

Abundant on lower-angle alpine routes, rock horns can provide solid anchors, provided that the rock is such that the sling won't flip off the top in the event of a fall. Using a slipknot may help keep the sling in place.

A horn slung with a slipknot

TRADITIONAL CLIMBING

Although the carabiner here is loaded tri-axially, (weakening it,) in this case it provides the most secure placement, keeping the sling in place

Passive protection

Passive protection (aka. without moving parts) rely on a bottleneck constriction in the crack to be held in place.

Nuts

Also called chocks or wires, nuts are the standard piece of passive protection, a must on every leader's rack. For a nut to be solid, it must be in a clear constriction in good quality rock that resists a downward and ideally outward pull as well, and have full contact with the rock on both sides. If the nut doesn't fit quite right, try flipping it 180° or use a different size.

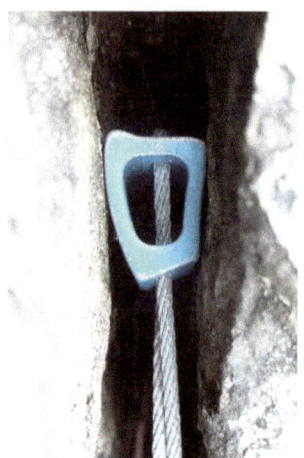

A good nut placement with complete contact on both sides

Nuts can also be placed along their wider axis, albeit a weaker placement due to less contact with the rock.

A nut placed sideways

If necessary, give the nut a solid tug downwards to set it so that it doesn't become dislodged as you climb past it, (although tug it too hard and your second will curse you as they struggle to remove it).

TRADITIONAL CLIMBING

Semi-active protection

Semi-active protection is protection that still depends on some (maybe modest) constriction in the rock, but also has some camming action so that the piece will twist under load, generating friction against a more parallel-sided crack.

Hexes

The original nuts had a hexagonal shape, as they were simply machine nuts with the threads filed out by innovative Welsh climbers. Modern Hexes have an asymmetrical shape that allows them to be placed in 3 different orientations. Like nuts, a good hex placement relies on solid contact between it and the rock on both sides. To use it in a semi-active manner (often in horizontal cracks), place it so that the sling is above the direction of pull. When placed correctly, under load, this will cause the hex to twist itself even more securely into the crack. Hexes are much lighter and less expensive that comparably sized cams.

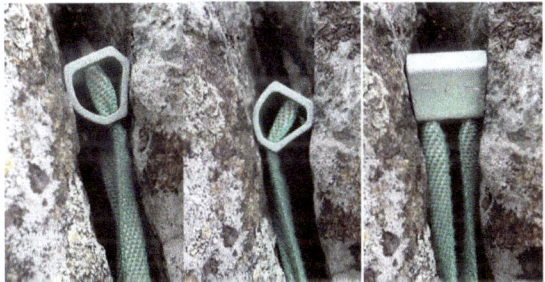

A hex placed in all three possible orientations, ordered by size. The middle orientation offers the most aggressive camming action.

Tricams

Tricams work great in horizontal cracks or in shallow pods that aren't wide or deep enough for a cam. The two rails on one side and the monopoint on the other must be in complete contact with the rock. For the placement to be stable, find a subtle indentation in the rock to hold the monopoint. Tricams can be easily dislodged from rope drag, so set them well, tugging sharply downwards and clip them with an extended sling (more on rope drag soon).

A good tricam placement in a horizontal crack. The monopoint is held in place by a divot and the two rails are in complete contact with the rock.

Whether to place the tricam with monopoint up or down will depend on which orientation offers the most secure placement. Start by feeling both sides of the crack/pocket with your fingers to find the best divot to hold the monopoint.

Tricams can also be placed in a passive orientation like a nut, although they are weaker than a similar-sized nut due to their reliance on a small pin attaching the sling to the tricam.

A tricam placed in a passive orientation

Sliding Ballnuts

Sliding ballnuts (or simply ballnuts for short) are small nuts with a moving brass ball that expands when the piece is loaded. For thin parallel

TRADITIONAL CLIMBING

seams, ball nuts are the only thing that works (besides pitons or aid gear like cam hooks and microcams). Since brass is a softer metal, the crystals and texture of the rock will deform it causing it to bite the rock and provide enough initial friction for the ball to open and the nut to expand into the parallel crack. For a ball nut to be solid, it must have complete contact on both sides (a deep enough crack with uniform walls). A ball nut is rated for much higher forces than comparably sized micro-nuts or micro-cams designed for aid-climbing.

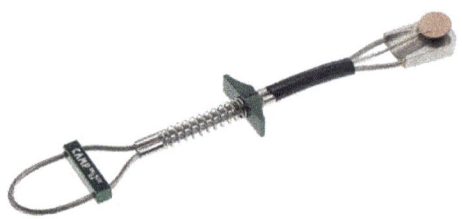

A sliding ballnut

Active protection – Cams

Spring loaded camming devices (SLCDs), "friends," or simply "cams", revolutionised free climbing in the 1970s as it finally became feasible to protect parallel sided cracks with one hand (instead of banging in pitons with a hammer).

Cam physics

A cam works by transferring the downward force of a fall into an outward force as the lobes of the cam rotate and push against the rock. Thanks to the friction between the cam lobes and the rock, the larger the downward force, the more the lobes will push outwards against the rock, exerting about twice the initial force on each wall of the crack.

Because of the shape of a cam lobe, based on the logarithmic spiral, the angle between the center of the axel and the point of contact with the rock remains constant. What this means practically speaking is that a cam will retain the same strength, transferring twice the force to each wall, regardless of how much the cam is retracted in its range.

The logarithmic spiral is often found in nature, for example in the shell of this Nautilus, a marine mollusk

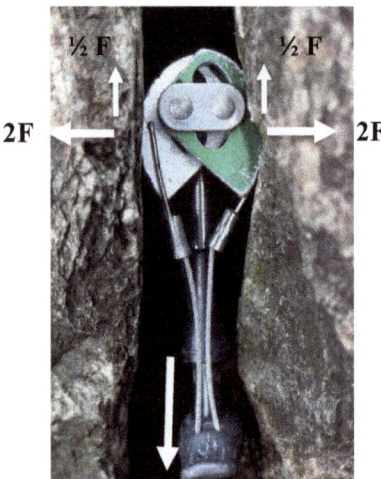

Downward force (F)

There are many different cams on the market, brilliantly designed with innovative features as well as trade-offs. Cams may have three or four lobes. Four-lobed cams are generally more stable and put less pressure on the rock (because there is more contact). However, three-lobed cams have a narrower profile and will often fit in places where a four-lobed cam won't (like pin scars) and are lighter. Cams may have a single or double axle design. A double axel gives the cam a greater range but increases its weight. The cam may have a single central stem, or two outer stems. A single stem makes the cam head more compact allowing it to fit in narrow placements. Older cams may have rigid stems which if loaded in the wrong direction (as for horizontal cracks) could snap or create sufficient leverage to pull out the lobes. The more flexible the stem, the more efficiently the downward force can be transferred into an opening of the lobes, even when the stem is not aligned in the direction of pull.

There exist several specialty cams on the market such as offset cams that will fit into flaring cracks, fat cams with wider lobes that increase the surface area in contact with the rock and thus decrease the pressure on soft rock types such as sandstone, link cams which will fit in a wide range of crack sizes, and totem cams which can hold even in shallow or uneven cracks.

Placing cams

When placing a cam, the first thing to look for is good macro rock quality. A cam more than any other piece of protection will generate extremely large forces. A cam can rip off a seemingly solid flake. A cam works well in a perfectly parallel crack. If the crack is slightly flaring, it may hold, but the placement quickly becomes marginal. A slight constriction (like slotting it in from the side) can make the cam bomb-proof but could also make it less secure if it walks. Cams (especially with four lobes) tend to walk upwards and deeper into the crack when rope drag wiggles them. This means that if the crack becomes wider behind the placement, the cam could walk back until the lobes are totally open and the placement useless. Therefore, perfectly parallel cracks are often the most secure, because even if the cam walks or pivots, the lobes will remain sufficiently retracted for the placement to retain its strength. If the crack is not uniform, look for the largest opening in the crack (like a pod) to place the largest cam possible. This way if the cam walks or pivots, the lobes won't open up.

A cam should be placed at least halfway retracted through its range, with both sets of lobes compressed equally. Although cam physics says that an under-cammed placement is just as strong, if it pivots or walks at all, the lobes may open up entirely and render the placement marginal. Place the biggest cam possible in a given crack, all the while being careful not to totally over-cam the piece, which makes it difficult for the second to clean. In a vertical crack, place the cam with the stem in the expected direction of pull. A cam in a vertical crack with the stem pointing straight outwards may pull as the lobes rotate before opening. In horizontal cracks, flexible stems are making these placements more and more secure, although fall on a cam in a horizontal and you may permanently kink your stem wire.

The holding potential of a cam relies on having enough initial friction for the downward force to be transferred into an outward one. This means that a seemingly good placement may pull if the walls of the crack are slick and untextured. Certain climbing areas are notorious for having seemingly good cam placements pull due to insufficient friction. Wider lobed cams may be useful here, or simply place passive chocks instead. Likewise, wet, dirty, mossy, or icy rock will provide less friction. The texture of granite crystals is perfect in providing the initial friction necessary to hold the cam. However, if the crystals become too big, be careful that the placement is not relying entirely on the integrity of such a crystal. Like with tricams, if the crystal or pebble breaks off, the entire placement may fail. Clean your cams regularly and use lubricant on the springs to keep the lobes moving freely. The spring-loaded rotation is essential to provide the initial friction needed to hold a fall.

Be sure that all the cam's lobes are in full contact with good-quality rock. Take your time to find the best placement possible. Small adjustments may be all that is necessary to make the best use of the rock quality at the micro level.

TRADITIONAL CLIMBING

A good cam placement, depressed halfway through its range

A piton tied off with a girth hitch. In this case, a carabiner could also be clipped through the eye of the piton to prevent the girth hitch from sliding off.

Fixed gear

Sometimes a route will be home to fixed gear. This could be a bolt, an old piton, or a fixed nut that a previous party failed to retrieve. Treat all fixed gear with caution as evaluating gear placed by someone else is always more difficult than that which you place yourself. Bolts should be modern (with a minimum stem diameter of 3/8 inches) not rusted nor moving. To know the quality of a piton you need to have pounded it in with a hammer yourself and judged it based on the increasingly high-pitched ringing as it went in. Without a hammer it is impossible to truly judge its quality. If it is rusted and old-looking it is probably not worth clipping. Repeated freeze-thaw cycles can severely weaken a piton placement. If it moves, likewise, you can probably pull it out with a good tug. However, good fixed pitons do exist. If the piton is only driven in partially so that the eye is not flush against the rock, leverage could cause it to pull out. Instead of clipping the eye, use a slipknot or a girth hitch to sling the piton instead.

A resident fixed nut can be bomber. It is often fixed because it held a leader fall and became permanently stuck in the rock. Make sure there is good contact and that the wire isn't too rusted.

If you decide to clip a piece of fixed gear, because of the uncertainty of its quality, back it up when possible with another bomber piece.

Protecting wide cracks (big bros)

If climbing offwidths is your thing, big bros (expandable tubes) may be your only choice of protection. For cracks between 10-15cm, they are lighter and more stable than equivalently sized cams. Commercially made cams (with the exception of the Valley Giant) go up to 15cm, whereas big bros go up to 50cm! Back in the day, wide cracks were protected by hammering in wooden pegs and planks, or they simply weren't protected at all. Big bros were invented in the late 1980s and provide relatively secure wide protection.

To place a big bro, find a parallel section of the crack, press one side of the tube against the rock, (the inner tube,) pull the trigger so it expands, wiggle it around to find the most stable placement and then screw the collar shut. Give it a good tug to test it, and if necessary, retighten the collar. Be sure to place it in the orientation such that the upward progress of the rope would tighten and not loosen the collar.

TRADITIONAL CLIMBING

A big bro placement in a wide crack

Practise placing these on the ground before jumping on the lead. They may take some fiddling to get a secure placement.

Leading on gear

Leading on gear is an all-encompassing challenge; climbing through hard moves while keeping the mental calm necessary to continuously evaluate the situation and make countless decisions with every movement. One must determine the immediate sequence of moves, deal with larger scale route-finding, decide when and how much protection to place - placing enough to make a fall safe when necessary, all the while conserving enough gear for higher up on the pitch, deal with rope drag, imagine secondary pulls, consider how the gear will not only protect oneself through cruxes and traverses, but also how it will protect the second, making sure the gear placed is easily removable by the second, and all without getting pumped!

When to place protection and how much

The primary concern is when and how much gear to place. The two main factors that will influence your decisions are 1. the likelihood of a fall and 2. the consequence of a fall. At all times a leader must be aware of the consequences of a fall and climb accordingly. Furthermore, add to the equation the possibility of the last piece of protection pulling and evaluate the result of such a situation. Then, balance this with the probability of a fall occurring. If the climbing is easy and the rock secure, it may be justified to run it out keeping in mind that a fall would be catastrophic. However, if there is even a modest chance of a fall, it is a good idea to keep at least two pieces of reliable protection between you and an injury. Placing more gear is obviously safer, but keep in mind that any gear you place lower down on the pitch you won't have later on. Try to conserve pieces in a variety of sizes for the end of the pitch, you may need them.

If possible, try placing protection from a solid stance, instead of in the middle of a hard sequence, which wastes precious energy.

Protection quality

When placing protection, its quality can be judged by three criteria in order of importance: its strength, its security and its ease of removal. Strength refers to its strength in the direction of the primary pull, security refers to its ability to resist a secondary pull from rope drag, and ease of removal refers to the amount of time it will take the second to clean the piece.

Strength

If a piece of protection isn't strong it is obviously marginal by definition. The placement may be bad due to poor contact and fit or questionable rock quality, or the piece itself may be marginal, rated to only a few kN such as small cams and micro-nuts like brass RPs.

Equalising protection

If the protection is marginal, you can find strength in numbers. Placing two or three

TRADITIONAL CLIMBING

questionable or small pieces and then equalising them to share the load can result in a reliable mini-anchor. Two (or even three) pieces can be equalised easily with one hand using a sliding X. Note that extension-limiting knots are impractical to tie on the lead.

To build a sliding X with one hand is as easy as "clip, twist and clip"

Equalising two pieces with a sliding X

To build a sliding X on three pieces, add a half twist (in either direction) in each of the two inner loops, then clip both inner loops and the outer one all together.

Three pieces equalised with a sliding X

Shock-absorbing quickdraws

Another strategy to deal with insufficiently strong protection is to clip it with a shock-absorbing quickdraw (also called a screamer). This is a long full strength (22kN) loop of sling, stitched weakly back on itself like an accordion. Although screamers differ between manufacturers, generally at about 3kN, the stitches begin to rip and the draw extend, absorbing energy and keeping the peak impact force experienced by the protection at a reasonable level. If you can't find reliable gear and the climbing above looks difficult, you might decide to clip your best piece with a screamer to increase the chances of it holding a fall. However, using screamers shouldn't replace finding quality protection!

TRADITIONAL CLIMBING

A screamer clipped to a marginal nut placement

Security

The security of a placement refers to its strength over a range of directions of pull.

Primary and secondary pull

The primary direction of pull is that which the piece will experience if fallen on as the top piece. This will always be primarily downwards but will also have an outward component. When falling, the climber often travels downwards in an arc, pushing away from the rock at the beginning of the fall and then swinging back towards it as they are caught by the rope. This means that the very initial force the piece experiences may be a weak outward one as the climber travels downwards past it before it becomes a strong downward force.

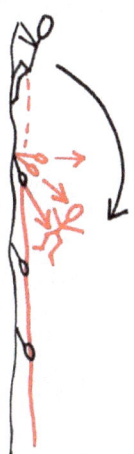

The primary pull on the top piece begins as an outward pull as the falling climber pendulums, then becomes a downward pull

The secondary pull is the direction of pull caused by rope drag. In the event of a fall, the upper-most piece will be pulled in its primary direction, but all the lower pieces of gear will be pulled by the rope in their secondary directions of pull such that the rope forms the straightest line possible. A good rule of thumb is that the secondary pull will be in the direction (horizontal component) of the next piece of protection placed. More precisely, if we consider three placements, the one before and after the piece in question, and draw an imaginary line between the previous protection placed and the future piece to be placed, the secondary pull on the piece in question will be perpendicular and towards this line.

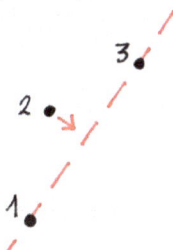

The piece in question (2) experiences a secondary pull towards the line running between placements 1 and 3

143

TRADITIONAL CLIMBING

Therefore, if after placing a nut, the route traverses left to the next piece of gear, while the primary pull on the nut will be downwards and outwards, the secondary pull will be to the left. The nut must then be able to resist a force in all of these directions.

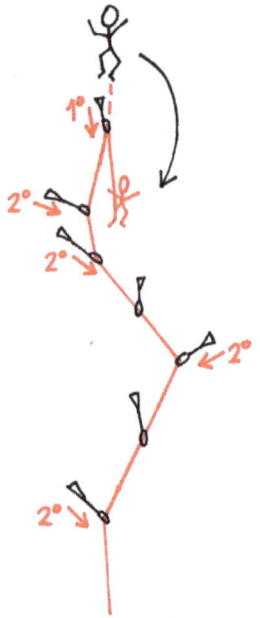

The secondary pull is caused by rope drag and is generally in the direction of the adjacent gear placements

What complicates matters is that the direction of secondary pull that a piece will experience is only determined once the subsequent piece of protection is placed. What this means is that when deciding whether to place a piece, you must consider where the route goes next and where the next placement will likely be in order to estimate secondary pulls.

Multidirectional placements

Ideally, all placements would be multidirectional, retaining their strength regardless of the direction of pull. A good cam in a parallel crack may be, as even if it twists upwards it keeps its integrity. Passive protection however relies on a constriction and so loading it in the opposite direction will likely dislodge it.

Opposing nuts

Two unidirectional pieces (often nuts) can be placed in opposition, each holding the other in the desired direction of pull, to make a multi-directional placement. This is useful in a vertical crack where the nut is strong for a downwards force but not an outward one. Likewise, opposing nuts in a horizontal crack may be the only possible protection if the crack is not deep enough to accept a cam or tricam, and since constrictions will be to the right or left, a single nut placement wouldn't hold the primary pull.

Start by clipping one of the two pieces with a 60cm sling, pass the sling through the carabiner of the second piece, back through the sling, then around the carabiner a second time. Pulling it tight, the friction of the sling will keep the nuts under tension.

TRADITIONAL CLIMBING

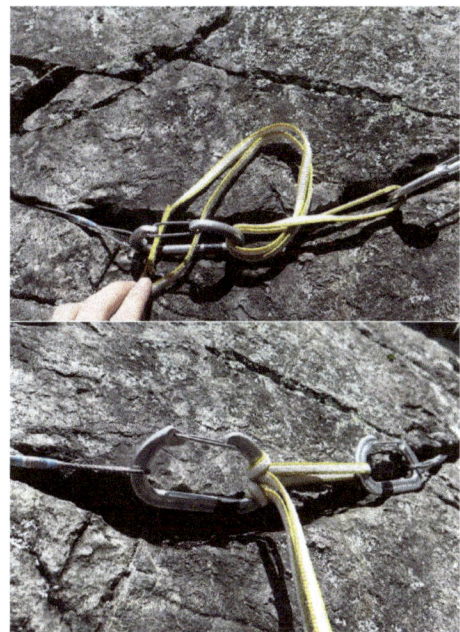

Alternatively, nuts can be held in opposition using clove hitches.

Two nuts clove hitched in opposition

Horizontal opposing nuts provide a multi-directional placement

Although the pulley effect will increase the force on the second piece, the friction of the sling will make this only marginally so. Likewise, the friction of the sling will greatly reduce the amount of force felt by the first piece. In vertical crack, the bottom piece should always be clipped first. In a horizontal crack, the strongest piece, that can also resist a slight outwards force should be used as the second, and the more finicky unidirectional piece should be used as the first.

Rigging with clove hitches is a good way to hold two pieces in opposition, but is more time consuming and difficult to do with one hand.

Extending placements (alpine draws)

The easiest way to improve the security of a placement is to clip it with a long quick draw. "Alpine draws" (extendos) can be extended to their full 60cm (or even 120cm) to reduce rope drag and minimize the secondary pull.

To set an alpine draw using a 60cm sling, pass one carabiner through the other, then clip it back onto two strands. To extend it, unclip a carabiner, then reclip it to any one strand.

TRADITIONAL CLIMBING

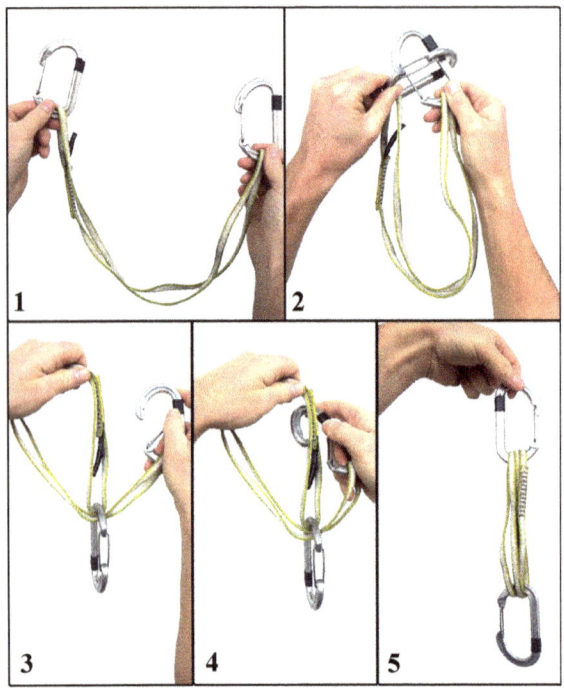

Shortening a 60cm sling to create an alpine draw

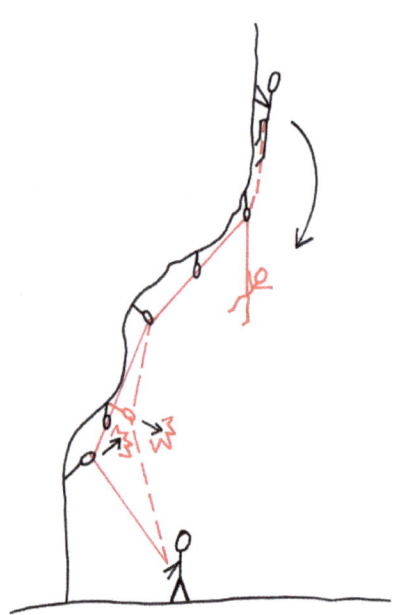

Zippering occurs when the bottom pieces fail to resist an upward/outward secondary pull

Alpine draws should largely replace short pre-sewn quickdraws on a trad climber's rack and can be clipped either in their short or extended forms.

Zippering

Zippering refers to the protection pulling one after the other from the bottom up, like a zipper opening. It has happened before, that an entire pitch of seemingly good nut placements all zippered out resulting in catastrophe. The next time you're climbing a sport route in the gym or outside, take your partner tight and study the direction in which the quickdraws are pulled. In sport climbing, bolts are multidirectional, but nuts are not. If the belay is not flush against the wall, the direction of pull of the first piece of gear will likely be outwards and upwards, especially for an overhanging route. If the piece can't resist a force in this direction, it will fail and the zipper will continue up the pitch until reaching a piece that can resist an upward pull.

To prevent a zipper, make sure the first piece on the pitch is multidirectional, either a good cam, a tricam in a horizontal, or opposing nuts. If this isn't possible, place a unidirectional piece to protect a fall and carry on, but place a good multidirectional piece as soon as possible. The problem is not just at the beginning of a route, but at any point where the steepness of the route increases and the rope bends, obviously from the ground to the wall, but also from a slab to a head wall. The last piece of gear on the slab and first piece of gear on the headwall should then be able to resist an upward pull as well. If the belay is positioned close to the wall and the wall is a slab, then there will be no major bend in the rope at the first piece and so a zipper is unlikely. Another way to think of it is that the rope will pull the pieces in a way so that it runs in the straightest possible line. Any gear that is distant from this line will be pulled towards it.

TRADITIONAL CLIMBING

Traverses

The general rule is that the primary direction of pull is always straight downwards (plus slightly outwards as the falling leader pendulums down). However, a fall on a traverse will pull the outer two pieces together, (imagine a top rope anchor).

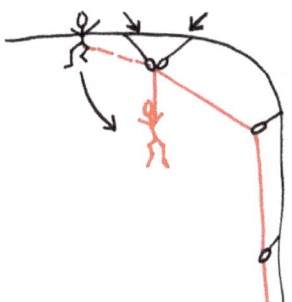

Thus, when placing protection on a traverse, make sure it is strong in a down and inward direction as this will be the primary direction of pull.

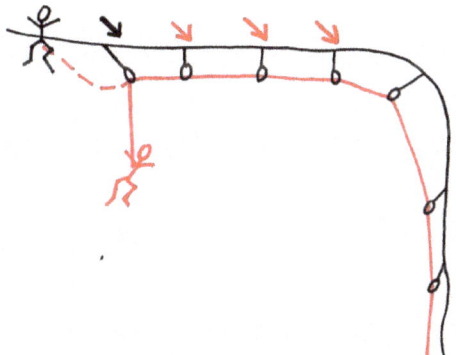

Leader fall on a traverse. Black arrows represent the direction of the actual primary pull on the last piece, red arrows represent the direction of a hypothetical primary pull on a piece if it were to catch a fall as the last piece.

However, for the second, the contrary is true: their fall will pull the last piece in an outward direction.

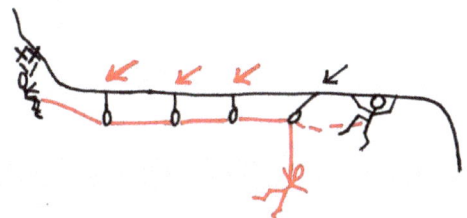

If the second falls, the direction of primary pull is now in the opposite direction

Ideally, multidirectional pieces like cams are used in a traversing section, but otherwise, try to place gear in groups of two like mini top rope anchors, the first to protect the second, the second to protect yourself.

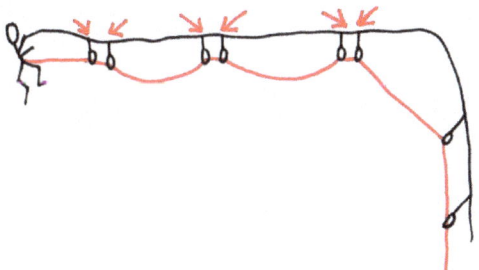

Gear is placed by the leader in twos, the first protecting the second, the second protecting the leader

Ease of removal

A piece of protection may have been bomber to protect a leader fall, but if it takes the second 10min to remove, it might not have been the best choice. Nothing saps time and enthusiasm like having to fiddle around trying to remove stuck gear. Although it is sometimes important to vigorously tug on nuts to set them, only do so when it is necessary. Although a cam is better over-cammed than under-cammed, make sure that it remains retrievable. If you are worried about an already over-cammed cam walking deeper into the crack, clip a long sling to it to reduce rope drag and prevent it from getting totally stuck. If there is an important piece of information to know about how

TRADITIONAL CLIMBING

to retrieve a piece of gear, for example if it was slotted in from one side or the other, make sure to tell your second.

When removing protection, before tugging on it, first observe it and determine how the piece went in by looking for the widest opening in the crack. Premature tugging could get the piece stuck for good. For nuts, it will often suffice to hold the attached draw and give it a good yank upwards. Don't pull too hard or you risk kinking the nut's wire. If this doesn't work, use your nut tool (which should be carried by both partners) to gently tap the nut upwards. Wiggle it back and forth to dislodge it from the constriction. If a piece is really stuck, you can use the nut tool along with an old carabiner (generally the one attached to the tool) or even a rock like a hammer and chisel. The heavier carabiner the better, so keep your tool on an old clunker. However, if you damage the nut this way it should be retired.

A nut tool

A nut tool can also be used to pull the trigger wires of a cam that has walked deep into a crack that you can no longer retrieve with your fingers. It can also be used to open a bottle of beer.

Rope drag

Rope drag, friction working against the upward progression of the rope, can be a serious problem. Friction is generated by the rope rubbing against the rock as well as through the pieces of protection. Every time the rope bends through a carabiner, there is significant friction added to the system, the amount increasing drastically with an increasingly sharp angle made by the rope. A long meandering pitch combined with a few lower placements creating bends in the rope can result in a seriously scary situation where it becomes effectively impossible to continue climbing without hauling up the rope with each step. Especially since long pitches often finish on easier, poorly protected slab sections leading to a ledge, excessive rope drag at the end of a pitch can result in dangerously long leader falls.

Furthermore, during a fall, rope drag can result in pieces lower down pulling as they are loaded in their secondary directions of pull. If the upper piece were to fail, the leader could then be falling a long way down.

Extending placements

As already mentioned, the simplest way to reduce rope drag is to clip protection with longer quickdraws. This is necessary when the piece would otherwise create a significant bend in the rope, and/or if the piece is less secure than desired in the direction of the secondary pull. Short "alpine draws" may be extended to use the full 60cm sling, or even a full 120cm sling may be used to reduce rope drag. The trade-off with over-extending protection is a longer fall.

Back cleaning

A piece of protection that will create horrible rope drag later on in the pitch may be necessary to protect a hard move. Having passed the move and placed another piece above, it may be worthwhile to down-climb enough to remove the piece. This is called "back cleaning".

Placing less gear

If a pitch is long (40m or more) and wandering, a good strategy may be to run out the beginning of the pitch placing less gear. A bend in the rope of a given angle will produce more rope drag overall the lower it is on the pitch. If the climbing is easy, you could choose to run it out. Even so, if on a multi-pitch climb, be sure to place at least two good pieces early on to avoid a factor 2 fall directly on the belay anchor. Alternatively, a safer solution may be to break the long pitch into two to make the rope drag more reasonable without sacrificing protection.

Protecting the second

Inexperienced leaders will obsess over protecting a potential leader fall but will forget to consider the consequences of a second's fall. During a traversing section, the second is just as exposed as the leader. Whereas a leader will intuitively place gear before a hard crux move on a traverse, they must also place a good piece afterwards to protect the second. Similarly, after topping out after a vertical section, before traversing right or left to build your belay anchor, be sure to place a directional piece for the second above to prevent a severe pendulum swing.

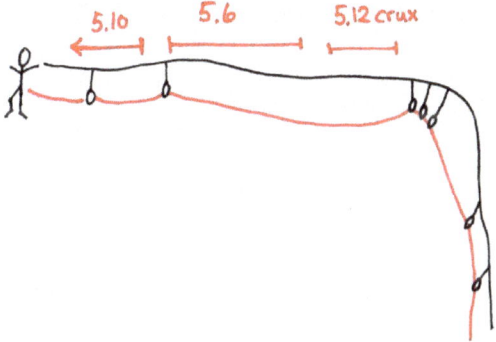

The leader protects the crux with three pieces of protection. Although well-protected for the leader, seconding this pitch would be dangerous.

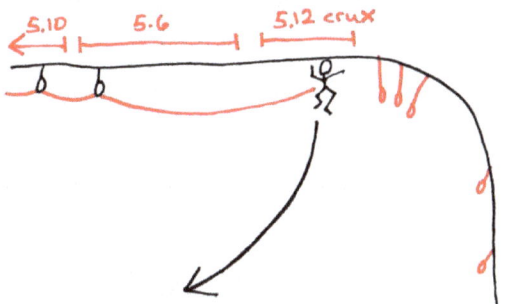

Throughout the crux, the second is exposed to a dangerous pendulum swing

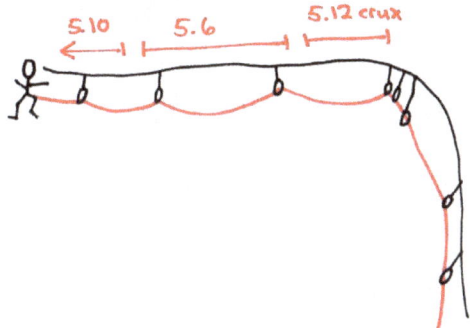

A well-protected traverse, both for the leader and the second

Leading with double ropes

Climbing with double ropes has many advantages. As well as being a lightweight option of carrying enough rope to do 60m rappels, double ropes make it possible to place multiple pieces widely spaced in a horizontal crack, to pull up slack to clip a high piece all the while staying protected by the other rope, to better protect the second and to more safely protect a wandering pitch while minimizing rope drag.

Although manufacturers recommend clipping the two ropes in strict alternation, it is common practise to keep one rope clipped on the right and the other on the left regardless of the frequency of protection on each side. Imagine a

TRADITIONAL CLIMBING

route that follows two vertical parallel cracks, a couple meters apart. If gear is placed in both, clipping each rope to only one line of gear will keep the ropes running straight without having to drastically extend the protection. Good rope management is important however, as crossed ropes could potentially sever in a fall, running over each other under tension.

Avoid clipping both ropes into the same piece of protection (unless they are also rated as twin ropes, which are intended to be clipped together). Double ropes are rated to have a certain elasticity and transmit a maximal force to the protection when used independently. When used together, the rope becomes essentially half as elastic and will transmit significantly more force to the system. Likewise, twin ropes should never be clipped independently (like double ropes) as they will be too elastic and insufficiently strong. Be particularly careful to avoid clipping two double ropes into the same protection carabiner after having clipped them separately in lower pieces. The difference in friction experienced by each strand will cause them to pull through the upper piece at different speeds and rub against each other generating heat and abrasion that could damage the ropes.

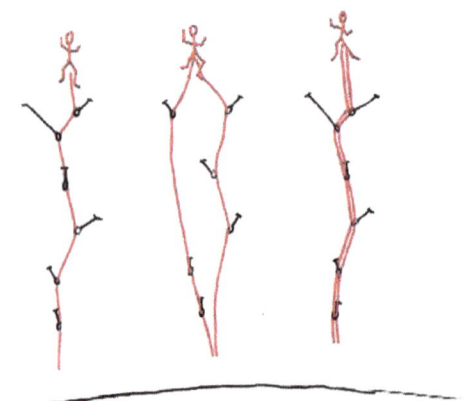

Single rope   Double ropes   Twin ropes

Note that for twin and single ropes, the protection is extended to decrease rope drag

Route finding

One of the great joys of trad climbing is the adventure involved in navigating the best way up. However, climbing off route, following holds or misleading chalk marks that lead to nowhere, or gunning for what you thought was a good gear placement that turned out to be a mirage, can result in a stressful situation. Throughout the entire pitch, you should be constantly evaluating the route at both the micro and macro levels. Every time you find a rest, take the time to lean back from the rock and consider where you want to be going. Being proficient in down-climbing is an essential skill to have as you may need to reverse the moves when you find yourself off route without protection.

The Rack

The rack a leader chooses to carry will depend on many particulars of the route including the rock type, crack width, length of the pitch, whether the belay is bolted, etc. More experienced leaders may be able to get by carrying less gear by being creative with their placements, but a beginner should always carry more than enough to protect the pitch. A standard rack may include:

- 1-2 sets of wired nuts
- 2-3 larger hexes
- 2-3 smaller tricams
- 1-2 sets of cams ranging from 14-88mm
- 8-12 quickdraws (at least half of them extendible alpine draws)
- 3-4 extra carabiners
- 1-2 120cm slings
- Anchor gear (one for single-pitch, two for multi-pitch)
- A nut tool to remove gear placements

Scope the route from the ground to determine the gear you'll need. Every pitch is different. Unless you're trying to onsight the route, read guidebooks, forums and talk to locals about what gear to bring.

Advanced belaying

A good belay can be the difference between a marginal piece pulling or holding. To decrease the forces experienced by the gear, belay as dynamically as possible (provided that the extra distance the leader falls doesn't result in a collision with a ledge, the ground or yourself). When catching a fall with a traditional belay plate or tube device, let a good 20-40cm of rope slip through the belay device, lengthening the fall but softening it. (Note that this is done by gently allowing your brake hand to be pulled towards the device during a catch, and not by allowing the rope to slip through your brake hand. Always maintain a firm grip on the brake strand.) Avoid belaying with a Grigri or other assisted-braking belay devices which increase forces due to the sudden braking action. To help enhance the security of the protection and prevent zippering, belay as close as possible to the first piece of gear to prevent it being pulled outwards and upwards in the event of a fall.

The strict ethics of British climbers (which prohibit the use of bolts despite minimal protection possibilities on the short but good quality Gritstone routes) have resulted in the perfection of advanced belay techniques that can turn an impossibly dangerous route into a somewhat safe ascent. A thorough preparation not only on the climber's part but also on that of the belayer, leads to a clear and lucid set of expectations. The rope is measured to assess the consequences of falling off at different points of the climb, and plans are devised in advance of what to do in such situations. Low on the route, extensive use of crash pads and spotting apply techniques from bouldering to route climbing. Higher up, if a fall occurs when the leader is far above the last piece of protection and risks a ground fall, the attentive belayer can dash backwards (or even jump off the belay ledge) in order to quickly take up slack and reduce the length of the fall. To prevent a zipper, a directional piece can be placed at the bottom of the route at the height of the belayer to hold an outward/upward pull. At all times the belayer is completely attentive, managing the amount of slack in often two ropes simultaneously (double ropes), and is ready to react.

Without embarking on overly dangerous Gritstone-style climbs, we can apply advanced belay techniques to our everyday belaying, or at least the mentality that belaying can and should be taken as seriously as leading is.

Traditional belay anchors

Although some trad routes will be equipped with bolted belay stations, often you'll need to build your own from scratch. If the belay is on a good ledge, there may be a bomber natural anchor to use (a tree or boulder), but otherwise the belay anchor will be built on gear placements. A belay anchor is only as good as the individual anchor points, and for a gear anchor, the minimum number is three bomber placements. If any one is less than ideal, place a fourth. A belay anchor must be absolutely bomb-proof because if it fails, it's game over. If you cannot find adequate gear placements, either keep going in search of a better belay possibility or down-climb to a previous stance. To review the basic concepts of belay anchors, see Chapter 3 on top rope anchors.

Where to build your belay

With the absence of bolted belays, you have the choice of where to build your belay anchor. Suggested belay positions are often noted in guidebooks and route descriptions, but ultimately, the leader decides where to stop and belay. More experienced parties trying to climb fast may choose to climb longer pitches to reduce the number of belay transitions on a long route, but less experienced parties should stop earlier to decrease potential rope drag, ensure sufficient protection and facilitate communication. When considering a belay position, you should look for the following criteria in order of importance:

TRADITIONAL CLIMBING

- Crack systems or other features to provide sufficiently strong protection
- Protected from rockfall
- Good visibility and communication with the second
- A ledge or stance to increase comfort for the belayer and belay transition

In some cases, the absence of any ledges will necessitate a hanging belay. Build the anchor with an extra piece of protection for psychological comfort and look for small footholds which will at least take some weight off of your harness.

Rigging with the climbing rope

Traditionally, belay anchors were rigged with the climbing rope clove-hitched into gear placements. The belayer then belays the second directly off their harness belay loop. Using minimal gear, this method is fast and efficient. It however has several important disadvantages. First, it is only practical if the climbers are swinging leads. Since the belayer is part of the belay anchor, the second, having arrived at the belay, has no place to clip into. Furthermore, the pieces are poorly equalised, the load being held primarily by one piece, and if built in a horizontal crack, one piece failing would lead to an extension of the system and a shock load on the next piece of gear. Finally, escaping the belay safely would take much creativity since there is no masterpoint to transfer the climber's weight to. Although rarely the method of choice, you'll be happy to have mastered this art when you find yourself at a belay after a long pitch, without any slings or cord left.

An anchor rigged with the climbing rope

To better equalise the placements, especially for anchor points situated horizontally, you can bring the rope back between each point to your harness belay loop, fastening it to a carabiner with clove hitches. This elegant rigging technique is popular in the UK. Start by clipping the first anchor point, then clove hitch this rope to your belay loop. Repeat for each subsequent placement. Note that it is possible to tie two clove hitches on a single large HMS pear-shaped locking carabiner, (although this will reduce its strength since it will be loaded on several axes simultaneously). You can clove hitch the final anchor point to avoid coming back a third time to your belay loop.

TRADITIONAL CLIMBING

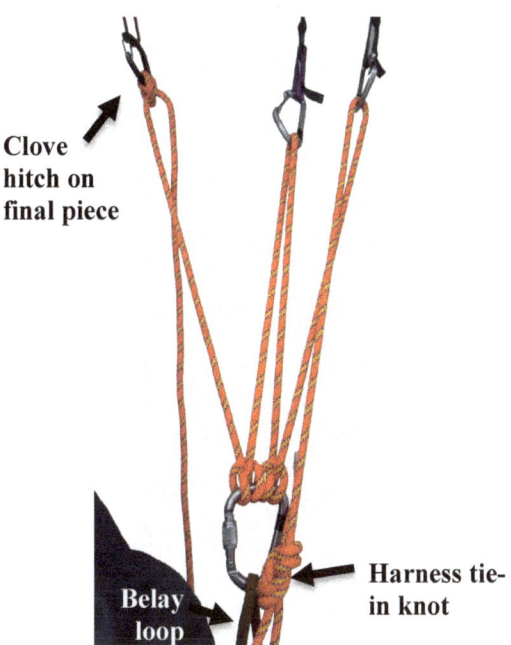

A better-equalised belay anchor rigged with the climbing rope

Because of the major disadvantages noted earlier, it's better to rig belay anchors with slings or cordelette so as to produce an independent masterpoint.

Rigging with slings

Anchors can be easily rigged with a collection of 60 and 120cm slings. If the anchor consists of three or more anchor points, a compound anchor (where two points are equalised to create an intermediate masterpoint which is then equalised with the remaining pieces) can be used to link all the pieces together. A mix of pre-equalised and self-equalising rigs may be used. Keep in mind however that the more complex the anchor, the more gear will be required to build it.

Trad climbers often carry dyneema instead of nylon slings due to their light weight. Remember that an overhand knot tied in dyneema reduces its strength by ~50%. Despite this, dyneema is still suitable for anchor rigging since 50% of a 22kN sling, 11kN, is sufficient per anchor leg.

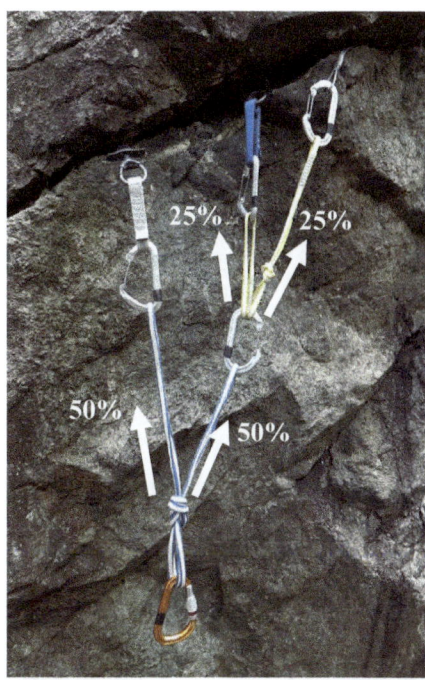

A compound anchor rigged with dyneema slings. The load is distributed 50:25:25. Even though an overhand knot reduces the strength of a dyneema sling by ~50%, this anchor can still withstand 22kN, 11kN from each major leg (50% of a 22kN dyneema sling).

A 3-point compound anchor will distribute the load unequally between the pieces, with each main leg receiving 50% of the load, further dividing in half at each equalised branch.

Note that the inner sliding X doesn't require redundancy since it makes up only one of two independent legs of the outer rig. Knots are therefore not required but may be useful to limit extension. If, like in the above example, one inner leg is short and the other long, it may be sufficient to tie only one extension-limiting knot in the long leg.

153

TRADITIONAL CLIMBING

Rigging with cordelette

The most versatile way to rig anchors is with a 6m strand of 7mm cordelette tied in a loop with a double fisherman's knot. Such a cordelette is usually perfect for rigging 3-piece anchors and can be doubled up to build 2-piece anchors.

Single-point anchors

If building a belay anchor on a single monolithic tree or boulder, simply wrap the anchor point, then tie a knot (overhand, figure 8 or figure 9) to create redundancy in the cordelette. If the cordelette is too long, begin by doubling it up.

Note that for a monolithic (single point) anchor, the shelf consists of clipping both strands of one leg and not one strand of each. **Never clip into the shelf of such an anchor without having the masterpoint clipped as well. Remember that a figure 8 can capsize when loaded at 180°.

Two-point anchors

A two-piece anchor is built usually on two bolts, but could be any two bomber anchor points including a nearly monolithic tree, a good chockstone or boulder, a perfect cam, etc.

The quad

When using a 6m cordelette, the best anchor to rig is the quad which is fast to tie, is self-equalising, and has two masterpoints to clip into. Begin by doubling the cordelette, clip the anchor point, tie two overhand knots, then clip the second anchor point. A masterpoint consists of clipping into any two strands between the knots. The quad is essentially the same as the sliding X, but because the cordelette (or sling) is doubled, there is no need to add the X and clip all strands at the masterpoint to create redundancy.

A single-point belay anchor built on a tree

TRADITIONAL CLIMBING

A quad anchor built on two bolts

Three-point anchors

When building belay anchors solely on rock protection, the standard is to use a minimum of three bomber pieces.

Pre-equalised cordelette

The simplest way to rig a three-point anchor is simply to clip all three with the cordelette, pull down all the strands and pre-equalise it in the anticipated direction of pull, then tie a knot to create a masterpoint. When belaying from above, the direction of pull will always be from the last gear placement in the pitch.

To prevent the double fisherman's knot from getting in the way, it is often helpful to begin rigging the anchor by clipping it to the first piece with a clove hitch.

1. Tie the cordelette to a piece using a clove hitch to isolate the double fisherman's knot, then clip the other anchor points

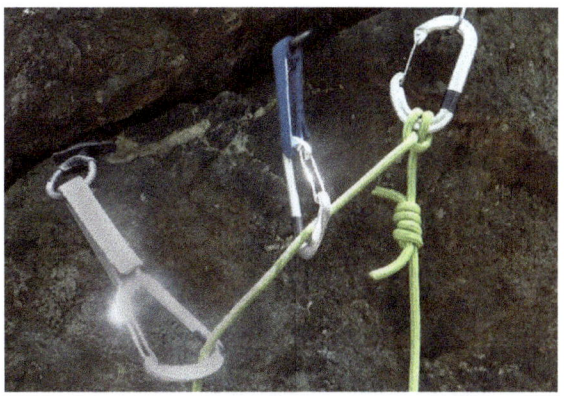

2. Pull down all strands to create three legs

3. Tie an overhand, figure 8 or figure 9 to create the masterpoint

TRADITIONAL CLIMBING

A well-built pre-equalised anchor should distribute the load equally 33:33:33 between the anchor points

A compound anchor combining a sliding X and a quad. The anchor is completely self-equalising and distributes the force 25:25:50.

Compound anchors

To distribute the forces unequally, you may choose to build a compound anchor by first equalising the two weaker pieces with a sliding X in a 60cm sling, then building a two-point quad with the cordelette.

Three-point equalette

The equalette is a variant on the sliding X or the quad, depending on whether the cordelette is doubled or not. The two major legs are self-equalising, each holding 50% of the force regardless of the direction of pull, and the anchor points within a major leg are pre-equalised using clove hitches. If the force is close to the anticipated direction of pull, the three-point equalette does a good job of distributing the load 50:25:25, and at worst, it will be distributed between two pieces, but never falling onto a single piece thanks to the self-equalising masterpoint. However, be aware of the potential shock load on the middle blue piece were the left piece to fail, discussed later in this chapter.

TRADITIONAL CLIMBING

A three-point equalette using a sliding X at the masterpoint. Note, an overhand knot is used to shorten the cordelette at the left-most piece. The load is distributed 50:25:25.

A three-point equalette using a quad at the masterpoint. Since the cordelette is doubled, the master point does not require an X. The load is distributed 50:25:25.

To tie an equalette, begin by locating the double fisherman's knot in the cordelette and isolate it by tying the two clove hitches to the two pieces within a major leg. Be sure that there is some slack in the cordelette between the pieces. Next tie the two overhand knots in the cordelette to determine the height of the masterpoint. After clipping the second leg of the anchor you may decide to tie an overhand knot to shorten the cordelette.

Four-point anchors

Building an anchor with four or more pieces takes a little creativity to be done logically and efficiently. If the four pieces are close together, the 6m cordelette may be long enough to build a simple pre-equalised rig.

A four-point anchor pre-equalised with a cordelette. The load is distributed 25:25:25:25.

If not, it is often easiest to start by equalising the two weakest points (sliding X with a 60cm sling), then building a pre-equalised three-point anchor. This way, each of the two weakest pieces hold only ~16.6% of the force.

A compound anchor combining a sliding X with a three-point pre-equalised rig. The load is distributed 33:33:16:16. Note how extension-limiting knots in the sliding X would be useless since the outer rig is pre-equalised.

If all pieces are of equal quality you may choose to build two initial sliding Xs and then equalise the two resultant masterpoints, (although this is probably unnecessarily gear intensive).

Four-point equalette

The four-point equalette does a good job at equalising all pieces. It is essentially a two-point self-equalising sliding X between two sets of pieces pre-equalised with clove hitches.

A four-point equalette. The load is distributed 25:25:25:25 and is self-equalising 50:50 between the two major legs.

As with a three-point equalette, begin by isolating the cordelette double fisherman's knot by first tying two clove hitches on one leg of the anchor. Continue by tying the two overhand knots on each side of the masterpoint, then finish by tying the last two clove hitches for the second leg.

Further notes on belay anchors

Distribution of forces

Anchors should be built keeping in mind the distribution of forces between the individual anchor points. If all pieces are equally strong, then the load should be distributed as equally as possible. However, if there are some placements that are clearly stronger than others, the anchor should be rigged such that the distribution of the load is proportional to the relative strengths of the individual pieces.

(The myth of) Equalisation

Self-equalising anchor configurations (the sliding X or quad) provide an efficient way to distribute a load between two pieces regardless of the direction of pull. Dyneema slings are better than nylon to shift and equalise the load when the direction of pull changes since the material is more slippery and generates less friction. Likewise, a quad does a better job at equalising than the sliding X since it creates less friction. Still, these self-equalising rigs are not magic, and an anchor will never be perfectly equalised. Tests have shown that at the moment of peak impact force, most of the load may be on one piece or the other. If one leg of a self-equalising anchor were to fail, the remaining piece must be able to withstand a shock load to avoid total anchor failure. The most important quality of a good belay anchor is not how it is rigged and equalised, but the strength of the individual pieces.

Consequence of anchor failure

When building a compound anchor, it is important to consider the consequences of one piece failing. The use of either pre-equalised or self-equalising rigs come with different strengths and weaknesses. The inherent trade-off between equalisation and extension means that although self-equalising rigs will distribute the load more evenly among the pieces, the failure of a piece could result in shock loading the remaining ones. Here we consider four configurations of a 3-point compound belay anchor. Black lines represent pre-equalised rigs and red lines represent self-equalising rigs (sliding X or quad).

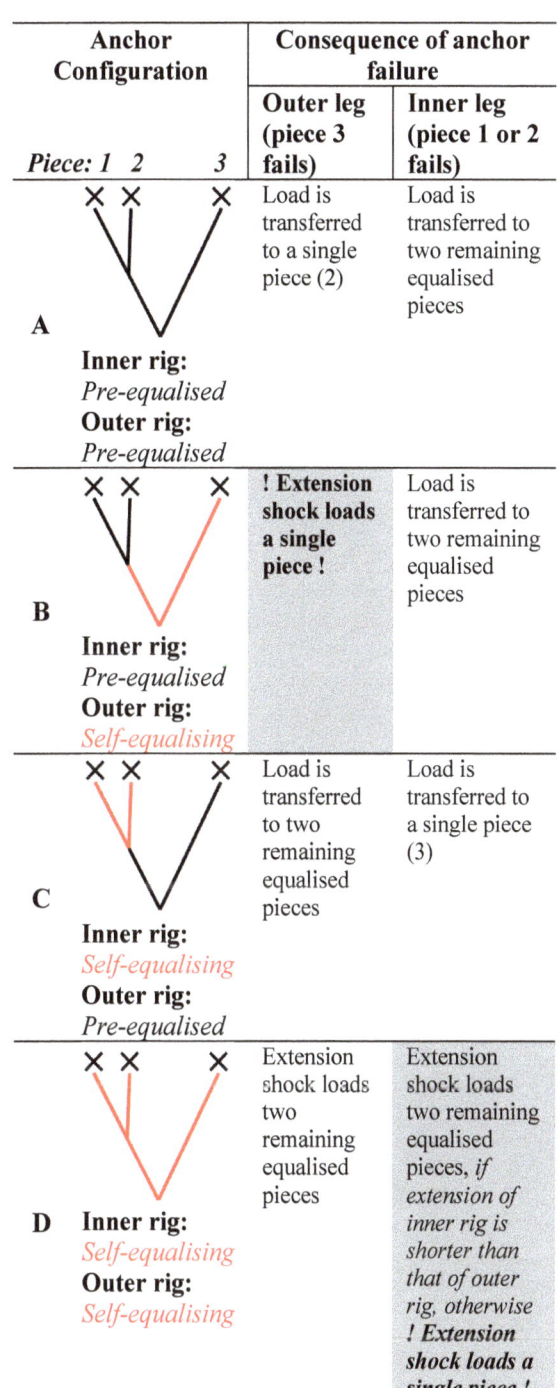

Consequence of anchor failure on remaining pieces for four 3-point belay anchor configurations. Black

TRADITIONAL CLIMBING

lines represent pre-equalised rigs and red lines represent self-equalising rigs (sliding X or quad).

Anchor configuration B, (for example a 3-point equalette) is potentially dangerous since failure of piece 3 results in a shock load on piece 2. Only rig such an anchor if all pieces are sufficiently strong to withstand shock loading. If not, place a fourth piece or at least rig more conservatively.

Anchor configuration D, a fully self-equalising compound anchor, can be potentially dangerous if attention is not paid to the position of the extension-limiting knots. To prevent shock loading a single piece which could result in subsequent and perhaps total anchor failure, tie extension-limiting knots such that the extension of the inner rig is shorter than that of the outer rig. The length of extension is determined by the distance between the extension-limiting knot and the masterpoint.

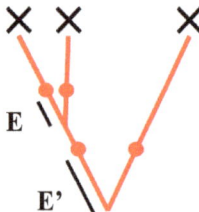

Extension-limiting knots in a fully self-equalising 3-point compound anchor. The extension of the inner rig (E) must be shorter than that of the outer rig (E') to prevent shock loading a single piece.

Multi-directionality

Although the primary direction in which a belay anchor must be strong is downwards towards the last piece of protection, once the next pitch is being led, a leader fall could pull the belayer upwards past the anchor. If the anchor is not built to withstand an upward force, there could be total anchor failure. Imagine a slung horn and a couple good nuts, that are bomber for a downward pull, but once pulled upwards, everything falls apart. An anchor built with a cam as the lowest piece will likely be multi-directional as it can swivel upwards and retain its strength.

If the lowest piece in the anchor isn't multi-directional, it may be necessary to place another piece of gear specifically to protect the anchor against an upward pull. If the piece doesn't need to be held under tension to maintain its integrity, it can simply be clipped into the masterpoint.

A belay anchor made multi-directional by an additional piece oriented for an upward pull, clipped to the masterpoint

If the upwards piece is far away, perhaps the simplest solution is to use the climbing rope to anchor the belayer using a clove hitch.

If the upwards piece needs to be held under tension (such as a nut), it must be rigged into the

TRADITIONAL CLIMBING

anchor cordelette. Begin by clipping the cordelette to the upwards piece, (a clove hitch will keep the knot out of the way,) then proceed by cinching it into opposition with the lowest downwards piece in the anchor as described earlier in this chapter. Once this is done, carry on with normal rigging.

Two pieces in opposition to reinforce the anchor for an upward pull

A fully multi-directional belay anchor. Note that the upwards piece is in opposition with the lowest of the three downwards pieces.

Independence

Although you may have built a seemingly perfect anchor on three good pieces in the same crack, if the crack, formed by a large block, opens up, then there is complete anchor failure. Unless the crack is a splitter "crack in the earth," the individual placements should be independent, in that they are not all dependent on the same rock feature. Use proper judgement.

V-angle

Anchor points that are too widely spaced will create an overly large V-angle unless the masterpoint is extended way beneath the pieces, which is often highly impractical. After having located the first couple placements, instead of

TRADITIONAL CLIMBING

looking right and left, clip them as lead protection and climb upwards a meter or two to find the remaining gear placement. Extend this with a long sling. If the V-angle is marginally too wide, you can reduce it by extending one of the pieces with a sling.

Cordelette stretch

Since cordelette is dynamic, the longer legs of an anchor will stretch more than the shorter ones. For example, if one piece of an anchor is placed just above the shelf in a pre-equalised anchor, whereas the other two pieces are in a crack a meter or so higher, the two longer legs will stretch much more. Despite being theoretically pre-equalised at 33:33:33, under load, the lower piece will end up taking the vast majority of the weight because its leg is more static.

Thus, when calculating the rough distribution of the load between anchor points, keep in mind that the lower pieces will take significantly more force than expected if using a dynamic cordelette compared to a static sling. To counteract this effect, begin by equalising the two lowest pieces and then use this masterpoint to build a compound anchor.

Alternatively, if only one piece is significantly higher than the others, begin by extending it with a long static sling before rigging the cordelette anchor. This will keep the different dynamic components of the legs of the cordelette similar in length.

Efficiency

A new leader will often take what seems like an eternity to rig a belay anchor at the top of the pitch. Although this is clearly better than quickly building a poor anchor, with time, a party will be able to save a significant amount of time on a multi-pitch route if belay anchors are chosen and rigged efficiently. Remember that the most important aspect of a belay anchor is not how it is rigged, but is the quality of the individual pieces. Start by locating the beginning of the next pitch, select your gear placements and then rig as quickly as possible. Always double check your work of art before calling "secure". If satisfied, trust your life to it, settle in on your ledge and enjoy the stillness of belaying as your partner struggles up the pitch to meet you.

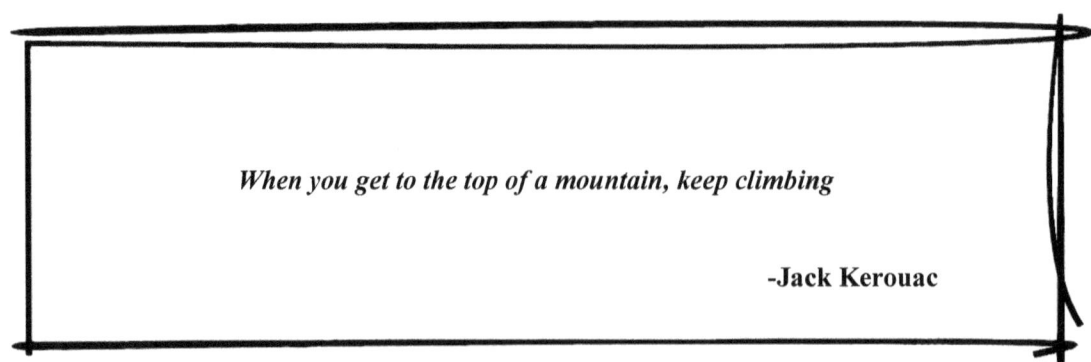

When you get to the top of a mountain, keep climbing

-**Jack Kerouac**

Appendix 1 – English-French translation of technical terms

English	*Français*
Aid climbing	Escalade artificielle, artif
Alpine draw (extendible quickdraw)	Dégaine extensible
Anchor point	Point d'ancrage
Assisted-braking belay device	Appareil d'assurage à freinage assisté
Autoblock (French prusik)	Nœud de Machard simple
Belay	Assurage, Assurer
Belay anchor	Relais
Belay chain	Chaîne d'assurage
Belay device	Appareil d'assurage
Belay loop (harness)	Pontet d'assurage (harnais)
Belay plate (belay device)	Appareil plaque-frein
Belay tube (belay device)	Tube d'assurage
Bolt	Ancrage permanent
Bolt hanger	Plaquette
Brake strand (belaying)	Brin de freinage (assurage)
Butterfly knot	Nœud papillon
Cam	Coinceur mécanique
Carabiner	Mousqueton
Catastrophe knot	Nœud de sécurité
Climbing	Escalade
Climbing shoes	Varappes
Clove hitch	Nœud de cabestan
Cordelette	Cordelette
Core (rope)	Âme (corde)
Counterbalance rappel	Rappel en contrepoids
Crash pad	Matelas d'escalade
Double fisherman's	Nœud de pêcheur double
Double-loop figure-of-8 on a bight	Nœud de lapin
Double ropes / half ropes	Cordes à double
Expansion bolt	Cheville à expansion
Fall factor	Facteur de chute
Figure 8 follow-through	Nœud en huit d'encordement/tressé
Figure-of-8 on a bight	Nœud en huit de plein poing
Fixed rope	Corde fixe
Flake (a rope)	Vraquer (une corde)
Flash	« Flasher »
Flat overhand (EDK)	Nœud de jonction simple
Flemish bend (reverse-threaded figure 8)	Nœud en huit de jonction tressé

Free ascent	Ascension libre
Friction hitch	Nœud autobloquant
Garda hitch	Nœud de cœur
Gate (carabiner)	Doigt (mousqueton)
Gear loops (harness)	Boucles porte-matériel (harnais)
Girth hitch	Tête d'alouette
Glue-in bolt	Scellement
Hangdogging	Travailler une voie
Harness	Harnais, baudrier
Hauling	Halage
Klemheist	Nœud de Machard français
Lead climbing	Premier de cordée
Leg (anchor)	Branche (relais)
Locking carabiner	Mousqueton verrouillable
Lower	Descente
Masterpoint (anchor)	Point-maître (relais)
MMO (Munter-mule-overhand)	Demi-cabestan mulé (Demi-cab–mule-simple)
MO (Mule-overhand)	Mule–simple (Nœud de mule sécurisé par un nœud simple)
Monster munter	Double demi-cabestan
Mule knot	Nœud de mule
Multi-pitch	Multilongueur
Munter hitch	Demi-cabestan
Nut	Coinceur (câblé)
Nut tool	Décoinceur
Onsight	Grimpe à vue
Overhand	Nœud simple
Personal tether (P.A.S.)	Longe, vache
Pitch	Longueur
Piton	Piton
PMMO (Prusik-Munter-mule-overhand)	Prusik débrayable (Prusik et demi-cab mulé)
Prusik	Nœud de Prusik
Quickdraw	Dégaine
Quicklink	Maillon rapide
Rappel	Rappel
Rappel rings	Anneaux de rappel
Red point	Enchaîner après travail
Rope	Corde
Rope drag	Tirage (friction)
Route	Voie
Screamer	Dégaine explosive/ amortissante
Screw-gate carabiner	Mousqueton à vis

English	Français
Self-rescue	Autosauvetage
Sheath (rope)	Gaine (corde)
Shelf (anchor)	Pont (relais)
Simul rappel	Rappel en simultané
Single-pitch	Longueur simple
Single rope	Corde à simple
Sling	Sangle
Slipknot	Nœud coulant
Spine (carabiner)	Dos (mousqueton)
Sport climbing	Escalade sportive
Stick clip	Pose-mousqueton
Stopper knot	Nœud d'arrêt (Nœud double)
Strop bend	Nœud plat
Swinging leads	Grimper en réversible
Tag line	Cordelette de récupération
Tandem rappel	Rappel en tandem
Tie-in points (harness)	Points d'encordement (harnais)
Top rope	Moulinette
Trad climbing	Escalade traditionnelle
Tramming	Technique du téléphérique
Twin ropes	Cordes jumelles
Water knot	Nœud de sangle
Webbing	Sangle (en vrac)

Appendix 2 – English-French translation of commands

English	Français
Climbing	Départ
Lower	Descente
Off belay	Corde libre
Off rappel	Corde libre
On belay	Assuré
Rock	Roche
Rope	Corde
Secure	Autoassuré / Auto
Take	À sec
That's me	C'est moi
Up rope	Avale

www.ingramcontent.com/pod-product-compliance
Lightning Source LLC
Chambersburg PA
CBHW051256110526
44589CB00025B/2846